Annual Survey

UK Government & Politics

Paul Fairclough
Eric Magee

Philip Allan Updates, an imprint of Hodder Education, part of Hachette UK, Market Place, Deddington, Oxfordshire OX15 0SE

Orders

Bookpoint Ltd, 130 Milton Park, Abingdon, Oxfordshire OX14 4SB
tel: 01235 827720
fax: 01235 400454
e-mail: uk.orders@bookpoint.co.uk

Lines are open 9.00 a.m.–5.00 p.m., Monday to Saturday, with a 24-hour message answering service. You can also order through the Philip Allan Updates website: www.philipallan.co.uk

© Philip Allan Updates 2009
ISBN 978-0-340-97283-0

First printed 2009
Impression number   5   4   3   2   1
Year   2014   2013   2012   2011   2010   2009

Printed by MPG Books, Bodmin

Hachette UK's policy is to use papers that are natural, renewable and recyclable products and made from wood grown in sustainable forests. The logging and manufacturing processes are expected to conform to the environmental regulations of the country of origin.

Contents

Chapter 1

Gordon Brown: back from the dead?

Context

For a brief moment in the autumn of 2008 it appeared as if the premiership of Gordon Brown had finally turned a corner. Following a year in which his party has been humiliated at the ballot box and both he and New Labour had hit rock bottom in the opinion polls, Brown had emerged as a leader of real stature — a man who could deliver Europe from the maelstrom of the deepening economic crisis. By the end of November, however, hope had dissipated once more with the publication of an ICM poll for the *Guardian* which showed Labour trailing the Conservatives by 15 percentage points.

This chapter charts the fluctuating fortunes of the prime minister in 2008. In so doing it will address questions such as:

- How was the prime minister faring as 2008 drew to a close?
- What factors had prompted the fleeting 'Brown bounce' in the autumn?
- Why has Brown found it so hard to make the step up from chancellor to prime minister?

How was the prime minister faring as 2008 drew to a close?

The closing weeks of 2008 saw the prime minister faring much as he had done back in January (see Box 1.1), despite the brief respite afforded by victory in the Glenrothes by-election on 6 November.

Box 1.1	Back where we started?

Voting intentions

	Labour	Conservative	Liberal Democrat	Other
January 2008	33%	41%	23%	8%
September 2008	24%	44%	20%	12%
November 2008	36%	40%	14%	10%

Who would make the best prime minister?

	Brown	Cameron	Clegg	Unsure
January 2008	27%	31%	5%	38%
September 2008	16%	34%	10%	40%
November 2008	31%	33%	7%	30%

Source: YouGov/*Daily Telegraph* tracker polls.

Indeed, the findings of the YouGov poll published at the end of November painted a rather rosier picture than was suggested in a number of other surveys published at or around the same time. In the ICM polls published by the *Guardian* and the *Observer* on 29 and 30 November, for example, the Tories held a 15% lead over Labour. More worrying for Gordon Brown and his party was the *Observer* poll's finding that 58% agreed with the statement that it was 'time for a change' — a view also shared, crucially, by a third of those who had voted Labour back in 2005.

Although poor poll ratings are a problem for any party in government, they are something of an occupational hazard for one in office so long. More problematic for Gordon Brown as 2008 drew to a close was the fact that Labour had fallen victim to another curse of long-serving governments; namely, a rather stale and uninspiring legislative agenda.

The Queen's Speech

As we have noted in our previous surveys, many of the major proposals that New Labour championed back in 1997 had — by the start of 2008 — either been completed or ended in stalemate: the former could be said to be true of the devolution programme in Scotland (particularly in the wake of the Calman Commission's report of 2 December 2008); the latter might easily be said to sum up a good deal of the party's constitutional reform agenda (e.g. Lords reform and electoral reform). Other policies had simply fallen by the wayside (e.g. elected regional assemblies in England) or seen their implementation slowed to such a snail's pace that one would need to sit still for a very long time in order to discern any tangible progress (e.g. ID cards).

The Queen's Speech of 3 December, therefore, provided an ideal opportunity for the prime minister to set out a clear legislative agenda for the 18 months that might remain in the current parliament, thereby recapturing the public imagination ahead of what will certainly be a fiercely contested general election.

In the event, while some of the bills outlined carried impressive titles (see Box 1.2), there was little that was truly ground-breaking. While it was true that measures such as the Saving Gateway Accounts Bill might make a genuine difference to those on the lowest incomes by supporting and rewarding their efforts to save, other initiatives were less impressive — even when they managed to capture the headlines. The Welfare Reform Bill, for example, was yet another effort to crack down on benefit cheats and the habitually workshy; the impressively titled Policing and Crime Bill proposed to tighten up the licensing of lap-dancing clubs and reform police authorities; and the Constitutional Renewal Bill (see elsewhere in this survey) passed over major constitutional issues in favour of a number of small and rather technical changes that were never likely to inspire a great deal of popular enthusiasm.

Box 1.2 **The Queen's Speech: much ado about nothing?**

- Banking Bill
- Borders, Immigration and Citizenship Bill
- Child Poverty Bill
- Children, Skills and Learning Bill
- Constitutional Renewal Bill
- Coroners and Justice Bill
- Equality Bill
- Health Bill
- Local Democracy, Economic Development and Construction Bill
- Marine and Coastal Access Bill
- Policing and Crime Bill
- Political Parties and Elections Bill (carried over from last session)
- Saving Gateway Accounts Bill
- Welfare Reform Bill

Source: www.guardian.co.uk, 3 December 2008.

In some areas, the proposals simply restated or simplified what was already there:

- The Child Poverty Bill simply enshrined in law the government's commitment to end child poverty by 2020.
- The Equality Bill simply brought together a number of existing anti-discrimination Acts and other instruments into a single bill.

In other areas, proposals appeared to offer changes that would, in all probability, make little difference to most citizens' lives:

- The Local Democracy, Economic Development and Construction Bill required local authorities to 'respond' to petitions.
- The Marine and Coastal Access Bill, among its other provisions, gives people the legal right to walk around the coasts.

Even those measures which appeared genuinely new — for example, the provision of a constitution of NHS patients' and staff members' rights and responsibilities — appeared to draw rather heavily on the Liberal Democrats' offer of an 'NHS guarantee' (see Chapter 5).

Options for Gordon Brown and his party

The 2008 Queen's Speech laid to rest the possibility that the prime minister would commit the government to 18 months of truly radical change ahead of what may well turn out to be a lengthy period in opposition for his party. That is not to say that all is lost, however, as a number of options remain for Brown and — more importantly — New Labour itself:

- **Muddle along and hope for the best.** There is no real reason why Brown should not remain in office until the spring of 2010. After all, as John Major proved in 1992 (if not in 1997), predicting the outcome of general elections is far from a precise science. There is always the chance that circumstances — and with them the relative fortunes of the major parties — can change.
- **Go for an early general election.** November 2008 saw speculation that the prime minister might take advantage of the so-called 'Brown bounce' and go to the polls in 2009. This would be a risky and somewhat surprising strategy given the fragile nature of the 'bounce' and the fact that the country is likely to be experiencing severe economic difficulties well into 2009.
- **Persuade the prime minister to step aside.** This is unlikely to be an easy task in the case of Brown, who had waited more than a decade for the top job, but it is less likely to result in long-term damage to the party than the final option (below).
- **Launch a formal leadership challenge.** Such challenges are always a messy business, although they can succeed in buying the governing party time and a little good will — as in the case of Margaret Thatcher's forced resignation in 1990. As a rule, it is generally better for parties to maintain a united front in the runup to such pivotal contests.

Although technically all four options remained 'in play' at the end of 2008, any attempt to usurp Brown is probably doomed to failure due to the dearth of possible replacements. The obvious candidates (e.g. David Milliband and Ed Balls) would be ill-advised to take on the role when their party is clearly in such a trough. To do so would be to risk the fate of William Hague, who replaced John Major in 1997 only to resign after the party's inevitable second consecutive general election defeat in 2001. Similarly, whereas younger cabinet members such as James Purnell might indeed harbour such lofty ambitions, a leadership bid in 2009 would probably represent a bridge too far (or at least too soon). The only realistic option, therefore, would be for a former cabinet member or an older statesman to step into the breach. Although many in the former category (e.g. Charles Clarke and Alan Milburn) have probably missed their political boat, some in the latter group (e.g. Jack Straw) might offer Labour a chance of stability, if nothing else. Straw was said to be keen to take on the role when Brown looked in danger earlier in his tenure.

What factors had prompted the fleeting 'Brown bounce' in the autumn?

The fragile 'Brown bounce' can be attributed to the following factors:
- **The faltering economy.** Although the public rarely re-elects a government that has presided over such a spectacular economic collapse, there is a natural tendency to rally around and 'stick with what you know' in the short term. The speed with which Brown and his chancellor Alistair Darling

moved to address the banking crisis also served to engender confidence in the government's ability to face down the markets.

- **Brown's record as chancellor.** The public perception of the prime minister's track record during more than a decade at the Treasury also served to bolster his position. Hard times call for stoicism and this is a quality Brown clearly has in spades. While even at the height of the crisis the polls had Cameron ahead of Brown as the person most voters would like to see in No. 10, the Brown/Darling double act invariably came out on top in polls targeting economic management. Significantly, however, even on the question of economic competence the Labour team's ratings were still far lower in November 2008 than they had been back in September 2007 (see Box 1.3).

Box 1.3 **A question of trust?**

September 2007

Who would you trust if Britain were in an economic crisis — Gordon Brown and his chancellor Alistair Darling, or David Cameron and his shadow chancellor George Osborne?

Brown/Darling	Cameron/Osborne	Neither/don't know
61%	22%	17%

November 2008

Who do you trust in the current economic crisis — Gordon Brown and his chancellor Alistair Darling, or David Cameron and his shadow chancellor George Osborne?

Brown/Darling	Cameron/Osborne	Neither/don't know
46%	33%	22%

Source: Ipsos MORI poll findings, September 2007 and November 2008.

- **Tory failings.** While there is something to be said for leading opposition leaders keeping their powder dry in times of crisis, it was generally agreed that the Conservative leader, David Cameron, and his shadow chancellor, George Osborne, did not make a good impression early on in the crisis. *Guardian* cartoonist Steve Bell, with his 'Torytubby' sketches, was not alone in portraying the Tory 'top two' as being more than a little naive at a time when Brown was championing the need for 'serious people' in these 'serious times'. The media coverage of meetings between George Osborne and the Russian oligarch Oleg Deripaska also impacted on the party's standing in the polls.

Although the 'Brown bounce' provided good copy for the broadsheets at a time when other stories were rather thin on the ground, one should remember that even at the height of this 'bounce', Labour and Brown were still trailing the Conservatives in the polls. Indeed, even in the same week that Labour was

cruising to victory in Glenrothes, ICM was completing the fieldwork for a *Sunday Telegraph* poll that would show the party to be a full 13 percentage points behind the Conservatives. Ultimately, therefore, Brown's autumn recovery was — to appropriate economic parlance — simply a 'dead cat bounce'.

Why has Brown found it so hard to make the step up from chancellor to prime minister?

Taking over from a leader as iconic as Tony Blair or Margaret Thatcher can never be an easy task, even where their departure from office has been so well received and so long in coming. Major, in truth, failed to stamp his authority on a party divided following Thatcher's fall from grace in November 1990, and Brown found it hard to impose his will on the Labour Party after Blair left the stage in the summer of 2007.

That said, while it is questionable whether or not any senior figure could have held the Conservatives together following the internecine conflict that had precipitated Thatcher's resignation, many of Brown's problems appear to be either a function of his own personality or a product of deficiencies in his approach to dealings with colleagues. While it is certainly true that the prime minister inherited a set of circumstances that he would not readily have chosen — not least a war on two fronts and a faltering economy — he took up the post with the benefit of a good deal of support and considerable political capital accrued during his time as chancellor. It is a mark of Brown's failure to engage with fellow MPs and with the broader public that the verdict we delivered on him a year ago (see Box 1.4) still largely holds true.

Box 1.4 | **Our initial verdict on Brown**

It is clearly far too early to judge just how effective a prime minister Gordon Brown may eventually become. What is clear, however, is that 10 years spent as chancellor — shielded from the full glare of media attention by a prime minister who revelled in it — has afforded the former chancellor little opportunity to develop the full range of skills he will need to succeed in the top job. Although the thoroughness and determination Brown demonstrated when chancellor have afforded him a certain amount of political capital, modern political leadership requires a clearer and more compelling vision than the prime minister has, as yet, been able to articulate.

Source: Paul Fairclough, Richard Kelly and Eric Magee, *UK Government and Politics Annual Survey 2008*, Philip Allan Updates.

Conclusions

It was tempting to see the prime minister as simply a victim of circumstance as 2008 drew to a close. If a leader's fortunes are indeed dependent upon 'Events, dear boy. Events', as Harold Macmillan once put it, then Gordon Brown's first 18 months in office had certainly been ill-fated (see Box 1.5).

That said, it would clearly be remiss of us to end our analysis there. It was Herbert Asquith who asserted that 'the office of the Prime Minister is what its holder chooses and is able to make of it'. While the premier's ability to succeed will inevitably be affected by the prevailing political context, it would be a mistake to ignore the importance of the part played by the incumbent's personal abilities and the abilities of those around the prime minister (both in office and in opposition) in shaping their destiny. While 2008 was indeed an *annus horribilis* for the prime minister, Brown's difficulties are — as we concluded in our 2008 survey — rather more deeply rooted.

Summary

- By the end of 2008, Gordon Brown and the Labour Party were faring little better in the polls than they had at the start of the year.
- The so-called 'Brown bounce' — widely attributed to the former chancellor's performance in response to the worsening economic situation — had quickly evaporated.
- The Queen's Speech had offered the prime minister a last chance to take the initiative and capture the public's imagination by launching a truly radical legislative programme ahead of a general election that was — at most — only 18 months away.
- The prime minister instead chose to offer a somewhat disparate collection of more modest proposals.
- Gordon Brown still appears to lack some of the skills considered essential in a modern prime minister, although the Labour Party's options are in truth limited: both by the prevailing political and economic climate; and by the dearth of suitably qualified and (crucially) willing rivals for his mantle.

Chapter 2

The 2008 London mayoral election: why did Boris beat Ken?

Context

Ken Livingstone's victory in the 1999 election for London mayor saw the official Labour candidate, Frank Dobson, pushed into third place: a notable early setback for a party whose decision to overlook Livingstone in favour of Dobson had prompted the former Greater London Council leader to launch his independent candidacy. In 2008 Livingstone — long since back within the Labour fold — was causing the party problems once more, losing the mayoralty to the Conservative challenger, Boris Johnson.

This chapter charts the course of the 2008 mayoral and assembly elections, identifying the main features of the campaign and considering possible consequences of Londoners' decision to return their first Conservative mayor. In so doing it will address questions such as:

- How did the major parties fare in the 2008 contest for London mayor?
- Why did voters reject Livingstone in favour of Boris Johnson?
- What does Johnson's election mean for London and for the Conservative Party?
- What can we learn from the 2008 elections to the Greater London Assembly?

How did the major parties fare in the 2008 contest for London mayor?

Around midnight on 2 May, a full day after the polls had closed, it was confirmed that the Conservative MP for Henley, Boris Johnson, had succeeded in his bid to defeat the Labour incumbent Ken Livingstone in the race to become mayor of London.

The result was more than a little ironic. Eight years earlier it had been Livingstone's victory as a rebel independent that had embarrassed the party. Now, with 'Red' Ken and New Labour long since reconciled, it was his defeat that caused angst. The result was also significant for the Conservatives, with Boris Johnson — a man whose candidacy had been regarded by many as something of a stunt at the outset — becoming one of the highest-profile Conservative politicians in the country.

Candidate	Party	1st pref.	% (+/−)	2nd pref.	%	Final
Boris Johnson	Conservative	1,043,761	42.5 (+17.9)	124,977	10.49	1,168,738
Ken Livingstone	Labour	893,877	36.4 (−0.4)	135,089	12.34	1,028,966
Brian Paddick	Liberal Democrat	236,685	9.3 (−6.0)	(641,412)	(26.11)	(878,097)
Siân Berry	Green	77,374	3.2 (+0.1)	(331,727)	(13.50)	(409,101)
Richard Barnbrook	BNP	69,710	2.8 (−0.3)	(128,609)	(5.23)	(198,319)
Gerard Batten	UKIP	22,422	0.9 (−5.3)	(13,651)	(4.63)	(136,073)
Andy Craig	CPA	39,249	1.6 (−0.6)	(80,140)	(3.26)	(119,389)
Lindsey German	LL	16,796	0.7 (N/A)	(35,057)	(1.43)	(51,863)
Matt O'Connor	END	10,695	0.4 (N/A)	(73,538)	(2.99)	(84,233)
Winston McKenzie	IND	5,389	0.2 (N/A)	(38,954)	(1.59)	(44,343)

Key: BNP: British National Party; UKIP: UK Independence Party; CPA: Christian People's Alliance; LL: Left List; END: English Democrats; IND: Independent.

Source: figures from www.bbc.co.uk, May 2008.

Table 2.1 London mayoral election (1 May 2008)

London mayoral elections operate under the supplementary vote (SV) system. Under this method, voters can cast both a first and a second preference. If no candidate secures an absolute majority of first preferences, all but the top two polling candidates are eliminated and their votes are redistributed according to second preferences (see Table 2.1). At the time of its introduction, it was felt that the SV system would favour Labour. Many in the party assumed that they would always be placed in the top two, alongside the Conservatives, on the basis of first preference votes and that they would do far better than the Tories when the votes of the Liberal Democrats and other eliminated candidates were transferred according to second preferences. In 2000, Livingstone's independent candidacy had split the centre-left vote, the result being that the official Labour candidate Frank Dobson finished in third and was eliminated. In 2004 and 2008, however, Labour certainly did benefit from second preference votes as anticipated.

Aside from Johnson's victory — and the collapse of the UKIP vote — the most notable feature of the 2008 result was probably the scale of the second preference vote for candidates who had no realistic chance of winning.

As we have seen, the SV system results in the elimination of all but the top two candidates, with their votes being transferred to second preferences. It would make little sense, therefore, for voters to cast their second preferences in favour of parties such as the Greens and the BNP unless they believed that these candidates were likely to finish first or second on the basis of first preference votes. The fact that both the Greens and the BNP secured significantly more second preference votes than first preferences therefore suggests that voters either did not understand the system in use or were using their second preference votes to make a statement (i.e. a 'protest vote'), knowing that it

would not affect the outcome. The latter would appear to be the more likely explanation, given that this was the third London mayoral election fought under SV. The 'protest vote' theory might also help to explain the performance of several other lower-placed candidates, particularly the one-time public face of Fathers4Justice, Matt O'Connor, whose English Democrats' candidacy secured only 10,695 first preference votes, while notionally picking up a further 73,538 votes on second preference.

Why did voters reject Livingstone in favour of Boris Johnson?

Johnson's mayoral candidacy was — as we have seen — regarded as something of a joke at the outset. Although the former editor of *The Spectator* and one-time shadow minister had made something of a name for himself as a television host since his return to the back benches in 2007, few had expected the member for Henley to contest the highest-profile directly elected position in the UK. As Matthew d'Ancona noted in *The Spectator*, however (see Box 2.1), Johnson was acutely aware of his public persona.

Box 2.1 Not simply a joke candidate

You don't hand London over to somebody just for a wheeze. Incumbency should never be confused with entitlement to office: a confusion that has been Livingstone's fatal error. But — equally — a desire to make mischief is not a sound reason to endorse a challenger. As Boris himself warned his admirers early on, a Mayor must be much more than a Bloody Good Bloke, a Pearly King of Japes.

Source: Matthew d'Ancona, 'Joking apart: why Boris is the man for the job', *The Spectator*, 26 April 2008.

For the incumbent mayor, Ken Livingstone, the biggest challenge was convincing the London public that it was not yet 'time for a change' at City Hall. Although Livingstone's appeal had always been that he was something of a maverick, it is hard to perpetuate the cult of the outsider when one has been in office for 8 years. Criticisms of the mayor's abrasive style (e.g. the disciplinary action he faced having accused a Jewish journalist of acting like a concentration camp guard), his policies (e.g. the congestion charge), and allegations surrounding the misuse of government funds — which later prompted the formation of Johnson's Forensic Audit Panel — all damaged Livingstone's chances in a campaign fought over a broad range of issues (see Box 2.2).

Box 2.2 'Candidates for London mayor get religion'

Transport, crime and the economy are traditional vote-winners, but places of worship are also battlegrounds in this year's mayoral election in London. The contenders have thrown themselves into photo opportunities and walkabouts in mosques, temples and churches as they realise the pivotal role of religion in the capital.

The mayor, Ken Livingstone, had his apparent epiphany last year in front of 50,000 Christians at a rally in Docklands. 'I realised you couldn't govern London without engaging with its religious communities...you can't get into office without their support.' Boris Johnson, the Conservative candidate, has celebrated the Sikh festival of Vaisakhi in Southall, toured a mosque frequented by the Dawoodi Bohra sect, had breakfast with the London Jewish Forum and visited a Hindu temple in Neasden.

Siân Berry, the Green candidate, said religion enjoyed a more pronounced role in this year's campaign because groups were better organised and had the ability to mobilise their flocks.

Source: *Guardian*, 28 April 2008.

Although Livingstone was quick to criticise Johnson's failure to plan properly or cost some of his proposals — not least the plan to reintroduce Routemaster buses — there was, in truth, little to choose between the candidates on policy (see Table 2.2). For some, the contest would ultimately swing on the issue of which candidate Londoners trusted most, with Johnson coming out on top according to one poll (see Box 2.3). Others, however, saw something more sinister in the contest. As Simon Heffer put it in the *Daily Telegraph* on 29 April, 'Mr Johnson is not a politician. He is an act. The same could fairly be applied to Mr Livingstone. Mr Johnson's act is, though, more finely wrought...It was decided, presumably by one of the advertising men who now control the Conservatives, that the only way to beat an act was with another, even better one. They certainly got the right man.'

	Livingstone	Johnson
Transport	£25 charge on most polluting vehicles. £500 m cycling and walking scheme. £16 bn Crossrail investment and tube modernisation. More travel discounts for OAPs, the disabled and students.	Scrap bendy buses in favour of eco-friendly Routemasters with conductors. Reform congestion charge. Scrap £25 tax on most polluting cars. Better cycle routes and safe cycle parking.
Housing	50% of new houses to be 'affordable', allowing more families to get on the property ladder.	Increase number of affordable homes. Encourage the building of more family homes with gardens. Protect historic views.
Crime	1,000 new police officers in the first year. Investment in youth clubs and activity centres.	More local community projects. £2.6 m on hand-held scanners and knife arches at transport hubs. New York-style maps of criminal hotspots.
Environment	Refit all public buildings to make them more carbon efficient. London-wide low emission zone.	Zero tolerance approach to littering and graffiti. London-wide low emission zone to improve air quality.

Source: *Guardian*, 19 March 2008.

Table 2.2 Ken versus Boris: how policies compared

Box 2.3 A question of trust?

'Do you think that Ken Livingstone or Boris Johnson will maintain the higher standards in public office?'

Candidate	%
Livingstone	37
Johnson	41
Don't know	13
Neither/other	9

'Do you think that Ken Livingstone or Boris Johnson is the more honest?'

Candidate	%
Livingstone	28
Johnson	38
Don't know	17
Neither/other	17

Source: *Guardian*, 3 April 2008.

What does Johnson's election mean for London and for the Conservative Party?

Johnson's ability to cause both amusement and offence in equal measure offered the prospect of a decidedly unpredictable mayoralty.

Many had come to regard Johnson's earlier gaffes — such as his comparing Tory leadership contests to ritualistic cannibalism and chief killing in Papua New Guinea — as being born more of naivety than any real malice. That said, there was still considerable debate as to whether his tenure as mayor would ultimately prove beneficial or detrimental to the Conservative Party's chances at the next general election. What was undeniable, however, was the fact that Johnson's victory marked a significant breakthrough in the capital, particularly when taken alongside the party's gains in the elections for the London Assembly (see below).

The Policy Exchange connection

Johnson's team in the capital was widely seen as a prototype for the next Conservative government, with those associated with the centre-right think-tank Policy Exchange well to the fore. Nick Boles, Johnson's chief of staff, was the group's former director. Johnson's director of arts, culture and creative leisure, Munira Mirza, was a Policy Exchange fundraiser and had also authored the group's pamphlet *Culture Vultures*. Interestingly, other former members of the group had also taken on key positions within the Conservative Party itself. Former Policy Exchange head of research James O'Shaughnessy, for example, had taken on the role of director of policy and research for the party. Although both Boles and O'Shaughnessy had severed their links with Policy Exchange, the axis between the former colleagues nonetheless appeared central to Conservative strategy as the party geared up for the next general election.

Johnson's policy agenda

Assessments of Johnson's first 100 days in post were mixed. In the *Guardian* on 8 August, the head of the London Group at the London School of

Economics, Tony Travers, concluded that 'unpredictable' was a good description of the Johnson administration, adding that 'there is a sense that anything could happen'. Critics doubted whether Johnson's attention span was equal to his obvious intelligence. David Cameron and Conservative Central Office were said to be in 'wait-and-see mode'.

Although the first 3 months of Johnson's tenure were certainly eventful (see Box 2.4), they were, as the *Guardian* noted, rather short on 'administration-defining announcements'.

Box 2.4 **Mayor Boris's '100 days'**

May

3   Johnson delivers victory speech.

5   Appoints Ray Lewis as deputy for young people.

7   Announces 'booze ban' on public transport.

8   Establishes Forensic Audit Panel to review Greater London Authority (GLA) Group spending.

9   Appoints former BBC journalist Guto Harri as communications director.

22 Appoints Tim Parker as his first deputy and chief executive of GLA Group.

25 Decides against renewing Ken Livingstone's oil deal with Venezuela.

31 Tube 'drinks party' on the eve of the 'booze ban'.

June

2   Cost of mayoral 'transition team' put at £465,000.

17 Asked to explain why the anti-racism message had been dropped from the Rise music festival, Johnson responds: 'Are you sure?'

19 Tells BBC Radio 4's *Today* programme that he 'doubts the existence' of a document designed to protect Londoners against spiralling cost of Olympics. Document is in fact on a government website.

22 Adviser James McGrath resigns after suggesting that elderly Caribbean Londoners 'go if they don't like it here'.

July

1   Announces consultation over congestion charge extension.

2   Holds press conference with Metropolitan Police chief Sir Ian Blair following knife murder.

3   Attends press conference and defends Ray Lewis against allegations of past financial and personal misconduct.

4   Lewis resigns.

5   Attends Gay Pride wearing pink Stetson.

16 Forensic Audit Panel report published.

21 Appoints right-winger Anthony Browne as policy director.

28 Announces rise in London living wage for GLA employees.

29 Revealed as having back-tracked on his policy that the Visit London website would only recommend employers paying the London minimum wage.

30 His deputy for policing, Kit Malthouse, said to have sought legal advice on power to suspend Sir Ian Blair.

August

5   Appoints Harvey McGrath as London Development Agency chair. Edmund Lazarus, who gave £22,250 to his election campaign, joins a board lacking a single Labour representative.

Source: *Guardian*, 8 August 2008.

Johnson's early policy initiatives largely failed to convince. On the eve of the introduction of Johnson's public transport 'booze ban' — a measure that had been well received on the whole — revellers organised a late night Tube drinks party that ended with nine people being assaulted (including four Tube drivers) and 17 arrests. According to the BBC, the general secretary of the Rail, Maritime and Transport Workers union, Bob Crow, said that 'Boris Johnson should apologise personally to all those who were assaulted and abused last night thanks to a half-baked gimmick designed solely as a publicity stunt and without a moment's thought for the people told to implement it'.

This suggestion that policy was being announced on the hoof, without proper planning or consultation, was hardly novel. During the mayoral campaign it had emerged that Johnson was not aware of the cost of buying the vehicles or recruiting and training the staff that would be needed to fulfil his pledge to replace Livingstone's bendy buses with the more traditional Routemasters.

In other areas of policy, critics questioned not only the mayor's planning but also his motivation. The Forensic Audit Panel — a supposedly independent body established on 8 May to review the spending of the Greater London Authority and the London Development Agency — was widely seen as an attempt to discredit the outgoing mayor. Such suspicions were fuelled by the fact that the head of the panel, Patience Wheatcroft, was a former editor of the *Daily Telegraph* and three of its remaining four members were active Conservatives. In a similar vein, while the circumstances surrounding the resignation of Johnson's deputy for young people, Ray Lewis, caused considerable embarrassment, the 'forced resignation' of the Metropolitan Police chief, Sir Ian Blair, on 2 October prompted more widespread concern, the suggestion being that the decision had been for political as opposed to operational reasons, with Blair widely seen as a Labour sympathiser.

As the year drew to a close, the remarks that Simon Heffer had made in the *Daily Telegraph* ahead of the mayoral election (see Box 2.5) appeared increasingly prescient.

Mr Johnson is the most ambitious man I have ever met. That ought to be a commendation for high office, since ambitious people normally understand they will go further only by doing their present job well. Mr Johnson's scattergun approach to life will not allow this.

The guiding theme of his life is the charm of doing nothing properly...Lynton Crosby, the Australian public relations guru who has kept Mr Johnson out of trouble during his campaign, returns home after it. Then what? Who will guide the unguided missile? Who will ensure that he turns up on time, or at all?

As Andrew Gimson [Johnson's biographer] makes clear, one of Johnson's failings is a belief that the public is there to serve him, not vice versa. He has given much pleasure to millions over the years, but will that cause the Underground to work better, the Metropolitan Police to catch more criminals, or business to thrive in London? Or would a Johnson mayoralty be yet one more chapter in an epic of charlatanry — perhaps, since it is so serious a job with potentially no hiding place, the last chapter?

Source: Simon Heffer, 'Why treat the London Election as a joke?', *Daily Telegraph*, 29 April 2008.

What can we learn from the 2008 elections to the Greater London Assembly?

Party	Seats	List		Total
		% vote	Seats	
Conservative	8	34.05	3	11 (+2)
Labour	6	27.12	2	8 (+1)
Liberal Democrat	0	11.22	3	3 (−2)
Green	0	8.29	2	2 (=)
BNP	0	5.33	1	1 (+1)
UKIP	0	1.90	0	0 (−2)
				25

Source: data from www.bbc.co.uk, May 2008.

Table 2.3 London Assembly elections (1 May 2008)

In truth, the elections to the Greater London Assembly probably told us little more than could be gleaned from an analysis of the various other electoral contests held in 2008. It was no real surprise, for example, that the Conservatives made gains in the assembly. Although London is not normally a happy hunting ground for the party, the Conservatives clearly benefited both from the 'Cameron factor' and from the desire of many to send a message to Gordon Brown and the incumbent Labour administration. Although the

Labour Party secured 27% of the vote and made a net gain of one seat compared to 2004, we should remember that the 2004 result was itself the product of massive protest voting 3 years into New Labour's second term in office.

A breakthrough for the BNP

More significant, perhaps, was the breakthrough for the BNP. The party has made steady inroads in the capital since 2005, following a decade in which its support base appeared to be firmly rooted in northwest towns such as Burnley and Blackburn. In the 2008 London Assembly elections, the party secured 5.33% of the popular vote across the capital, breaking through the 5% threshold that had prevented it from winning a seat in 2004, when it polled just 4.8%. As a result, the BNP secured its first seat in the 25-member assembly at the third attempt, with its failed mayoral candidate Richard Barnbrook returned from the party's list.

Although the BNP's success in 2008 may result in part from the economic downturn and concern over immigration, the style and focus of the party's campaign might also have contributed to its increased share of the popular vote. Ahead of the elections, the party had made a widely reported attempt to reach out beyond its regular core vote, in part by raising the profile of the party's few ethnic minority candidates and councillors. On 10 April, for example, the *Guardian* reported that the BNP was making a concerted effort to appeal to the Jewish community in the face of what it saw as the rise in militant Islamic sentiment in some parts of the capital. The paper quoted the party's only Jewish councillor, Patricia Richardson, who said that she was in the BNP 'because no one else speaks out against the Islamification of our country' and because being Jewish only added to her 'concern about this aggressive creed that also threatens our secular values and Christian tradition'.

The BNP's efforts to open a dialogue with the Jewish community (despite opposition from organisations such as the Jewish Board of Deputies and the London Jewish Forum), its open attacks on Islam and its pronounced support for Israel were all evidence of a rather more sophisticated and subtle electoral campaign than the party had managed in earlier contests.

Conclusions

Boris Johnson is both the highest-profile directly elected Conservative politician in the country and, it could be argued, the most powerful, possessing extensive executive powers and control over a budget in excess of £3.1 billion. Although early verdicts on the performance of the new mayor have been somewhat mixed, it remains the case that his performance over the next 12 months still has the potential to have a massive impact on his party's chances at the next general election, for better or for worse.

Summary

- Johnson won the mayoral election as a result of a number of interconnected factors: some relating to public perception of the two main parties at the time of the contest; some resulting from Ken Livingstone's performance in-post; or linked to Johnson's unique appeal.
- Johnson's position as the highest-profile and most powerful elected Tory politician and the fact that his team was so closely associated with those in charge of Conservative Party strategy meant that the fate of the mayor and the electoral fortunes of the party were seen as having a high degree of co-dependence.
- Johnson failed to make a mark on policy during his first 3 months as mayor.
- Some initiatives appeared poorly thought through and the administration was also rocked by a number of high-profile resignations.
- The major parties performed much as expected in the 2008 London Assembly elections.
- UKIP lost both of its seats and the BNP achieved a modest increase in its share of the popular vote, thereby securing its first ever seat in the 25-member assembly.

Chapter 3

2008 local and by-elections: lessons for New Labour?

Context

Although Gordon Brown's decision not to hold an election in October 2007 denied the public the chance to effect a change in government, 2008 brought numerous other opportunities for voters to make their views heard through the local elections, five separate by-elections, and the London mayoral and assembly elections. The latter were dealt with in Chapter 2. This chapter charts the electoral fortunes of the major UK parties in the various local elections and parliamentary by-elections held in 2008, identifying the salient campaign issues and considering whether Labour is really in a position to learn from its many defeats ahead of a likely general election in 2010. In so doing it will address questions such as:

- What problems was Gordon Brown's Labour administration facing in 2008?
- How well did Labour perform in the 2008 local elections?
- Why were there five by-elections in 2008?
- What issues were these by-elections fought on and what can we learn from the results?
- Is New Labour now incapable of winning the next general election?

What problems was Gordon Brown's Labour administration facing in 2008?

In an ideal world, Labour would have looked to avoid facing so many electoral contests at a time when the prevailing political and economic conditions were so unfavourable.

New Labour's appeal in 1997 had been threefold (see Box 3.1). Although the party's problems clearly started long before Gordon Brown became prime minister, the early months of 2008 were dominated by a series of developments that served to undermine further what had appealed to voters 11 years before. By the end of May 2008, Labour was experiencing its lowest poll ratings in the modern era, with just 23% backing the party.

In no area was this loss of public confidence more apparent than in the field of economic affairs. Although there was clearly some merit in Gordon Brown's contention that the UK was facing a truly 'global' credit crunch, the government faced criticism for its management of the UK economy in times of acute uncertainty.

- The party had succeeded in convincing the broader public that it could manage the economy competently, not least by distancing itself from the tax-and-spend approach adopted by earlier Labour administrations.
- It had promised to bring greater honesty and integrity to government, putting an end to the allegations of sleaze that had dogged John Major's Conservatives during their final years in office.
- Blair and his frontbench team had managed to project an energy and a sense of purpose that contrasted sharply with a Conservative administration widely regarded as too long in office and rather short of ideas.

Initially, considerable attention focused on rising fuel costs, with the government under pressure to suspend the fuel escalator, as it had in 2001 following the fuel protests. Much more damaging for the party was the battle over the move to axe the 10p tax rate — a decision that appeared to strike at the party's core support by disadvantaging those on the lowest incomes. With former Labour minister Frank Field and others on the Labour back benches making a Commons defeat on the issue a realistic prospect — and with the Crewe and Nantwich by-election fast approaching — the chancellor of the exchequer, Alistair Darling, was forced to offer a £2.7 billion raft of concessions. The prime minister's insistence that public sector pay deals should be pegged to below 3% similarly served to alienate the party's traditional supporters at a time when the official rate of inflation was well over 4% and fuel prices were rising at around four times that rate.

The cumulative effect of these decisions — following on from the earlier forced 'nationalisation' of Northern Rock — threatened to erode Labour's hard-won reputation for economic competence. It also risked bringing the party into conflict with the major public sector unions; this at a time when the withdrawal of many of Labour's wealthy donors had made the party more reliant on union funding than it had been at any time since the New Labour project began.

The issue of sleaze also dragged on into 2008, even though the police investigation into the alleged sale of peerages had concluded the previous July without charges being brought. The scandal surrounding the failure of some candidates in the 2007 Labour deputy leadership contest to account properly for donations to their campaigns finally claimed the scalp of work and pensions secretary Peter Hain on 24 January. Crucially, whereas the scandal surrounding Hain's campaign served to undermine Labour's reputation further, the alleged abuses of parliamentary allowances by Tory MP Derek Conway and others were, on the whole, reported as 'personal' rather than 'party' scandals.

The faltering fortunes of the prime minister, Gordon Brown, also served to undermine Labour's electoral efforts in 2008. Even at the time of the former chancellor's 'coronation' as leader in July 2007, there was disquiet among some

leading figures in the party. The prime minister's indecision over 'the election that wasn't' in October 2007 and his obvious discomfort in the media spotlight fuelled the growing feeling that Brown might not be the best person to lead Labour into the next general election.

Finally, the fact that so many contests happened in such quick succession in the 6 months between May and November 2008 also allowed the opposition parties the opportunity to build campaign momentum — what US commentators refer to as 'the Big Mo' — while affording Labour little time to take stock and revise its campaign strategy accordingly.

How well did Labour perform in the 2008 local elections?

It is not uncommon for the party in government to face heavy losses in local elections, as the Conservatives found to their cost between 1979 and 1997. Voters often regard such contests as an opportunity to register a protest vote — a chance to send a message to those in office at Westminster.

Therefore, although Labour losses in 2008 were to be expected, the results on 1 May still represented a bad night for a party hoping to keep losses down around the 200 mark (see Table 3.1). The final total of 344 lost seats was somewhat lower than the net loss of 505 sustained a year earlier, but it should be remembered that almost double the number of councils had been contested in 2007.

Party	3 May 2007: England				1 May 2008: England and Wales			
	Councils		Councillors		Councils		Councillors	
	Net +/−	Total	Net +/−	Total	Net +/−	Total	Net +/−	Total
Conservative	39	165	911	5,315	12	65	257	3,155
Labour	−8	34	−505	1,877	−9	18	−334	2,365
Liberal Democrat	−4	23	−246	2,171	1	12	33	1,804
Others	0	5	−162	1,112	−1	0	41	1,092
No overall control	−27	85	–	–	−3	64	–	–
	312 councils declared				159 councils declared			

Source: figures from www.bbc.co.uk, May 2007 and May 2008.

Table 3.1 Local election performance compared: 2007 and 2008

Such extensive losses brought to mind the problems faced by John Major's Conservatives during their final years in office. In the 1995 local elections, the Conservatives had polled just 25% of the popular vote, succumbing to a crushing general election defeat 2 years later. In May 2008, Labour had managed just 24% nationally at a similar stage in the electoral cycle.

Although attempts to extrapolate results in local elections onto a bigger electoral canvas are fraught with problems, such extensive losses would certainly have given Labour pause for thought: not least because those losing their seats in such contests are the grassroots activists upon whose shoulders falls the burden of organising the general election campaign at constituency level. Such reversals at the polls are not, therefore, simply about losing control of local councils: they can also represent a degrading of the local party infrastructure.

Why were there five by-elections in 2008?

Although by-elections in recent years have invariably resulted from either the death or the resignation of the sitting MP (see Table 3.2), the five contests that took place in 2008 came as a result of a number of different sets of circumstances:

- The Crewe and Nantwich by-election resulted from the sudden death of Labour MP and long-serving chair of the Transport Select Committee, Gwyneth Dunwoody.
- The vacancy in Henley resulted from the election of the incumbent MP Boris Johnson to the position of mayor of London.
- The contest in Haltemprice and Howden was prompted by the decision of the then Conservative shadow home secretary, David Davis, to step down on principle and re-contest his seat on the issue of civil liberties and the 42-day detention for terrorist suspects.
- The by-election in Glasgow East followed the decision of incumbent Labour MP David Marshall to resign due to ill-health.
- The vacant seat in Glenrothes resulted from the death of Labour MP John MacDougall, following his 2-year battle with mesothelioma — a form of lung cancer commonly associated with exposure to asbestos.

Constituency	Date	Cause
Cheadle	14 July 2005	Death
Livingston	29 September 2005	Death
Dunfermline and West Fife	9 February 2006	Death
Blaenau Gwent	29 June 2006	Death
Bromley and Chislehurst	29 June 2006	Death
Ealing Southall	19 July 2007	Death
Sedgefield	19 July 2007	Resignation
Crewe and Nantwich	22 May 2008	Death
Henley	26 June 2008	Resignation
Haltemprice and Howden	10 July 2008	Resignation
Glasgow East	24 July 2008	Resignation
Glenrothes	6 November 2008	Death

Table 3.2 By-elections, 2005–08

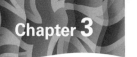

Haltemprice and Howden aside, however, the precise circumstances in which each of the vacancies arose had only a limited bearing on the contests themselves. Far more significant were the broader national trends identified earlier in this chapter, as moderated by the salient issues unique to each constituency.

What issues were these by-elections fought on and what can we learn from the results?

Crewe and Nantwich (22 May)

Despite the fact that the seat ranked as only the 210th safest Labour seat of the 355 that the party won in the 2005 general election, its loss to the Conservatives (see Table 3.3) marked a significant downturn in Labour's electoral fortunes. Although Labour had lost a number of such contests to the Liberal Democrats in recent years, the swing of 17.6% in Crewe and Nantwich represented the largest movement of votes from Labour to the Conservatives in a by-election since 1977.

Party	General election: 5 May 2005		By-election: 22 May 2008	
	Votes	%	Votes	%
Labour	21,240	48.8	12,679	30.6
Conservative	14,162	32.6	20,539	49.5
Liberal Democrat	8,083	18.6	6,040	14.6
Others	–	–	2,240	5.4
Turnout	60.3%		58.2%	
Swing	17.6% (Labour to Conservative)			

Table 3.3 Crewe and Nantwich by-election: Conservative gain

Commentators were quick to attribute Labour's failure in Crewe to the problems facing the party nationally, but it was clear that Labour's strategy in the constituency had also backfired badly. Although Labour's decision to put up Gwyneth Dunwoody's daughter, Tamsin, as its candidate was understandable, given the affection in which her mother had been held in the constituency, it smacked of nepotism. As David Cameron quipped during one of his four visits to the area during the by-election campaign, although we have a hereditary monarchy, we do not have hereditary MPs. Labour's efforts to brand the Conservative candidate Edward Timpson a 'Tory toff' — in particular, its deployment of Labour activists dressed in top hats and tails — were also poorly received by voters. Timpson was from a wealthy family, but he was seen as the local candidate — living only a short drive from the constituency. Dunwoody, in contrast, lived on a 5-acre holding in Wales and, as Jeremy Paxman pointed out, had her own entry in *Burke's Peerage*. Such realities hardly appeared to provide grounds for a class-based campaign.

Crucially, Labour's attempt to mitigate the damaging effects of the row over the 10p tax rate by offering a £2.7 billion raft of concessions failed to ease the haemorrhaging of votes in Crewe. The party's failure to offer a referendum on the Lisbon Treaty, the state of play in Iraq, the treatment of injured soldiers, and the ongoing dispute over police pay were also reported as being significant door-step issues in the constituency. Gordon Brown's decision not to visit the constituency during the campaign — although fully in line with the convention that prime ministers do not get involved in such contests — also brought criticism.

Henley (26 June)

Although the result was never really in doubt in a constituency made vacant by Boris Johnson's election to the post of mayor of London, the campaign in Henley was anything but anodyne. The Conservatives and the Liberal Democrats clashed over issues ranging from saving the local hospital to maintaining school budgets, with the issue of whether or not each party's candidate was really 'local' important once more, just as it had been in Crewe.

Labour was never expected to do well in such a staunchly Conservative seat, but this was the first time that Labour had ever finished behind the BNP in a parliamentary election and the first time since the end of the Second World War that the party in office had finished fifth in a by-election (see Table 3.4). Labour's humiliation in Henley hardly provided the most conventional way for Gordon Brown to celebrate the end of his first year as prime minister.

Party	General election: 5 May 2005		By-election: 26 June 2008	
	Votes	%	Votes	%
Conservative	24,894	53.5	19,796	56.9
Liberal Democrat	12,101	26.0	9,680	27.8
Labour	6,862	14.7	1,066	3.1
Green	1,518	3.3	1,321	3.8
UK Independence	1,162	2.5	843	2.4
British National Party	–	–	1,243	3.6
Turnout	67.9%		50.5%	
Swing	0.8% (Liberal Democrat to Conservative)			

Table 3.4 Henley by-election: Conservative hold

Haltemprice and Howden (10 July)

Conservative shadow home secretary David Davis had announced his intention to resign a day after the Counter Terrorism Bill, which extended the limit for the detention of terrorist suspects from 28 to 42 days, had passed its third reading in the Commons. The coverage Davis received in the media was largely positive, particularly so in the tabloids, but those around the Westminster village were less unanimous in their approval. David Cameron

was said to have seen Davis's gesture as counterproductive, although the Conservative Party leader publicly expressed admiration for his former colleague's integrity. Critics on both sides of the Commons regarded Davis's decision as somewhat premature, given the fact that the Lords had yet to pass the bill and that major legal challenges to the measure were also anticipated. Some wondered what Davis could possibly hope to gain by throwing away his shadow cabinet portfolio, just as his party appeared destined to return to office after more than a decade in opposition. A few regarded the whole episode as being rather self-indulgent on Davis's part, with the culture secretary, Andrew Burnham, even suggesting that Davis himself should cover the estimated £80,000 cost of organising the by-election.

Davis's decision to step down and re-contest his Commons seat on the issue of civil liberties resulted in an atypical contest. Not since Labour and the Liberal Democrats opted to give the anti-sleaze candidate Martin Bell a free run against Neil Hamilton in Tatton in 1997 had a parliamentary election on the UK mainland involved only one of the three main parties. In Haltemprice and Howden, however, Labour declined to field a candidate and the Liberal Democrats — who broadly approved of Davis's stand — also chose to step aside.

That did not stop others stepping into the breach, however, with 25 other candidates appearing on the ballot in scenes reminiscent of the recall election that saw Arnold Schwarzenegger first elected governor of California in 2004. Although many of these candidates were somewhat quirky (see Table 3.5), and only four aside from Davis secured more than 500 votes, it created an interesting spectacle nonetheless.

Crewe and Nantwich

Candidate	Party	Votes
'The Flying Brick'	Monster Raving Loony	236
Paul Thorogood	Cut Tax on Diesel and Petrol	118

Henley

Candidate	Party	Votes
'Bananaman Owen'	Monster Raving Loony	242
'Harry Bear'	Fur Play Party	73

Haltemprice and Howden

Candidate	Party	Votes
'Mad Cow-Girl'	Monster Raving Loony	412
Gemma Garrett	Miss Great Britain Party	521
David Bishop	Church of the Militant Elvis Party	44
Ronnie Carroll	Make Politicians History	29

Table 3.5 'Alternative' by-election candidates in 2008

Glasgow East (24 July)

The result in Glasgow East (see Table 3.6) was by far the biggest by-election shock of the season. Although the earlier resignation of the Scottish Labour leader, Wendy Alexander, on 28 July hardly helped the Scottish Labour Party's preparations, few expected anything other than a Labour victory in a constituency that had been Labour's 26th safest seat at the time of the 2005 general election, and its third safest seat in Scotland.

Party	General election: 5 May 2005		By-election: 24 July 2008	
	Votes	%	Votes	%
Labour	18,775	60.7	10,912	41.7
SNP	5,268	17.0	11,277	43.1
Liberal Democrat	3,665	11.8	915	3.5
Conservative	2,135	6.9	1,639	6.3
Others	1,096	3.5	1,431	5.5
Turnout	48.2%		42.2%	
Swing	22.5% (Labour to SNP)			

Table 3.6 Glasgow East by-election: SNP gain

Glasgow East is, in many respects, a natural Labour heartland — a seat where life expectancy is significantly lower than the national norm and unemployment was running at 1 in 4 at the time of the contest. One should remember, however, that the ballot in Glasgow East did not come in isolation, but at the end of a 3-month period where Labour had suffered major losses in the local elections, a chastening defeat in Crewe and Nantwich and a humiliating fifth place behind the BNP in Henley. To compound matters, the party's decision not to field a candidate in Haltemprice and Howden, far from taking the wind out of David Davis's sails, had only served to remind voters of the prime minister's loss of nerve when faced with the decision of whether or not to call a snap general election the previous autumn.

Such difficulties aside, further electoral embarrassment might still have been avoided had delays in selecting the party's candidate in the constituency not effectively gifted opposition parties a 3-day head-start in the campaign. The failure of the supposed front-runner, Glasgow councillor George Ryan, to appear at a selection meeting on the evening of 4 July was followed by his decision to withdraw from the race, citing family reasons. It was not until 7 July, therefore, that the party was finally able to confirm the candidacy of MSP Margaret Curran: reportedly its fifth choice.

What followed was a campaign fought not only on the issue of the economic plight of the constituency itself, but also on the performance of the Labour

government and its leader nationally, compared to that of the self-styled SNP government north of the border. Although Labour held a 14% lead over the SNP in an ICM poll taken on 14 July, things deteriorated badly thereafter. Despite the fact that Labour officials remained hopeful of a narrow victory on the eve of the election — fearing only that Labour supporters might stay at home — the party's candidate was ultimately defeated by a margin of 365 votes on a turnout that was actually far better than anticipated.

The aftermath of the defeat saw some in the media focusing on identifying possible explanations for the result, while others pondered on precisely where a uniform swing of a similar magnitude away from Labour at the next general election would leave the party: namely out of government with only 20 MPs. All were agreed, however, that 24 July was a bleak day for New Labour. As one anonymous MP remarked in the *Guardian* 2 days later, 'the problem for Gordon is that he now has a full deck of cards in terms of lost seats. He has lost in London, he has lost a Tory seat, coming fifth in Henley, he has lost in a Midlands heartland seat and he has lost in his own backyard. He has been rejected by every part of the country'.

Glenrothes (6 November)
The Glenrothes contest was unusual in that it had long been anticipated: the incumbent Labour MP, John MacDougall, had been fighting against an incurable form of cancer for over 2 years. Indeed, the SNP was even accused of running a low-level campaign in the constituency ahead of MacDougall's death on 13 August, a claim the party strenuously denied.

For Labour the question of precisely when to hold the resulting by-election was key. Although many had expected the contest to take place towards the end of September, such a date was problematic because it would have coincided with the party conference season. A crushing by-election defeat for Labour would have given succour to those hoping to hijack the Labour conference in order to spring a leadership challenge on Brown. Defeat a week later would have provided a fillip for the Conservatives as they opened their conference in Birmingham on 28 September. Although all of the major parties' candidates were in place by the middle of September, therefore, the anticipated polling date of 6 November was only officially confirmed in early October.

Labour sweeps to victory
The scale of Labour's victory in Glenrothes (see Table 3.7) came as something of a surprise, even to those who had confidently predicted a 'Labour hold' in the wake of the final round of polling. Although there was still a notional swing of nearly 5% from Labour to the SNP, the reality was that both parties had prospered at the expense of the Liberal Democrats, the Conservatives and others. The Liberal Democrats, in particular, suffered a spectacular collapse in support.

	General election: 5 May 2005		By-election: 6 November 2008	
Party	Votes	%	Votes	%
Labour	**19,395**	**51.9**	**19,946**	**55.1**
SNP	8,731	23.4	13,209	36.5
Liberal Democrat	4,728	12.7	947	2.6
Conservative	2,651	7.1	1,381	3.8
Others	1,861	5.0	712	1.97
Turnout	55.7%		52.3%	
Swing	**4.96%** (Labour to SNP)			

Table 3.7 Glenrothes by-election: SNP gain

Labour's success in Glenrothes can be attributed to three interconnected factors:
- **The faltering economy.** Although economic problems normally play into the hands of opposition parties, the opposite proved true in the UK in 2008. The prime minister's assertion that 'serious times call for serious people' appeared to tap into more widely held doubts regarding the Conservative frontbench team, while the media coverage of meetings between George Osborne and the billionaire Russian oligarch Oleg Deripaska saw the shadow chancellor's approval ratings fall from 90% to 7%. Alex Salmond's often stated desire to model an independent Scotland on countries such as Ireland, Iceland and Norway also took a hit as the crisis deepened: Ireland foundered; Iceland drifted towards bankruptcy; and Norwegian officials publicly called for the SNP leader to stop making comparisons they regarded as wholly erroneous. The cumulative result of this was a marked 'Brown bounce' in the polls, as voters shifted back towards the man so long associated with 'economic prudence'.
- **Local issues.** Although national issues clearly played their part in Glenrothes, their importance should not be overstated. As shadow Scottish secretary David Mundell noted, 'this was an election which was fought on very local issues, very Scottish issues'. On the ground, Labour campaigned hard on the alleged failings of the SNP-controlled local government in Fife (specifically the suggestion that it had cut school budgets and restricted nursing care for the elderly) and on the SNP's plan to introduce a local income tax across Scotland.
- **Brown's local connections.** Brown's personal connections with the area and his willingness to exploit such links also paid off. Labour's candidate, Lindsay Roy, was rector of Kirkcaldy High School, Brown's *alma mater*. The prime minister's decision to break with precedent and campaign personally in the constituency also played well with local voters.

More than anything else, the results in Glenrothes and Glasgow East provide an illustration of just how much the political landscape in Scotland has changed in recent years. Scottish voters now have two parties of government: Labour at Westminster and the SNP at Holyrood. As long as this remains the case, it is inevitable that assessments of the relative performance of these governments will shape future contests north of the border.

Conclusions: is New Labour now incapable of winning the next general election?

Although large swings, low turnouts and high levels of protest voting have long been a feature of local elections and parliamentary by-elections, the same is not true of general elections. In 2001, for example, the swing from Labour to the Conservatives was only 1.75% nationally, and in 2005 the figure was only a little higher at 3.05% — with only 62 seats changing hands.

Historically speaking, seats won on the back of large swings in by-elections are particularly hard to read, as such results are so often overturned at the very next general election. While a uniform swing of the scale seen at Crewe and Nantwich would result in Labour losing all but 44 of its Commons seats in a general election, such a shocking statistic only serves to highlight the inherent point-lessness in extrapolating the data from such a small and unrepresentative sample.

Statistics aside, it is clear that the series of setbacks suffered by the party in 2008 raises serious questions regarding Labour's future electoral prospects. Although Labour's victory in Glenrothes offered a brief respite, the ICM poll published in the *Sunday Telegraph* on 9 November (see Box 3.2) suggested that this victory was simply a short-term 'Brown bounce', rather than evidence of a more fundamental shift in national voting intentions.

Box 3.2 Testing times for New Labour in 2008

- **1 May:** Labour suffers a net loss of 334 councillors and 9 councils in the local elections, accompanied by defeats to the Conservatives in the London mayoral and assembly elections.
- **22 May:** Labour loses the Crewe and Nantwich by-election following a 17.6% swing to the Conservatives.
- **31 May:** a YouGov voting intentions survey puts the Conservatives on 47%, Labour on 23% and the Liberal Democrats third on 18%. This represents Labour's worst poll rating since records began.
- **26 June:** Conservatives hold Henley, with Labour trailing in fifth behind the Liberal Democrats, the Green Party and the BNP.
- **10 July:** Labour decides not to field a candidate against Conservative David Davis in the Haltemprice and Howden by-election.
- **24 July:** Labour loses Glasgow East following a 22.5% swing to the SNP.
- **6 November:** Labour wins the Glenrothes by-election, despite a notional 5% swing to the SNP.
- **9 November:** an ICM poll for the *Sunday Telegraph* puts the Conservatives on 43%, Labour on 30% and the Liberal Democrats on 18%.

From the time of its inception, the New Labour project was seen as having as much to do with developing and executing effective campaign strategies as with advancing a coherent ideological creed. Although Brown tried to regain the initiative with the appointment of Stephen Carter as his chief of strategy and principal adviser on 7 January, the former chief executive of Ofcom stood down in October in order to become broadcasting minister in the Lords, his 9 months in the post having manifestly failed to bring about a reversal of the party's fortunes in the face of forces that threatened to undermine the very things that had made the party so electable in 1997. While it is perhaps a little simplistic to draw parallels between Labour's predicament under Brown and the dog-days of John Major's Conservative administration a dozen years ago, the similarities are too obvious to dismiss entirely.

Summary

- Labour began the year having seen many of the things that had made the party so electable a decade earlier brought into question.
- The 2008 local elections were a huge setback for Labour with the party suffering a net loss of 334 seats and losing control of 9 councils.
- Labour fared poorly in the five parliamentary by-elections fought in 2008, losing two out of three of their own seats, coming fifth behind the BNP in a safe Conservative constituency, and declining to field a candidate in the other contest.
- Gordon Brown's new chief of strategy and principal adviser, Stephen Carter, proved unable to arrest the party's decline.
- Many commentators began to draw parallels between the beleaguered Gordon Brown and the last Conservative incumbent of No. 10, John Major.

Chapter 4

Civil liberties: do we live in a national security state?

Context

19 March 2008 saw the publication of the government's new National Security Strategy for the United Kingdom. This document, which came at the end of a decade of unprecedented challenges for the nation, sought to bring key elements of foreign and domestic security policy into a more coherent whole. For many, however, 2008 marked the point at which they started to question just how much liberty they were prepared to sacrifice in order to protect their freedom; whether the UK was, in fact, in danger of becoming a surveillance nation — a 'national security state'.

This chapter considers the implications of the government's new strategy in the context of the ongoing domestic and global threats to UK security. In so doing it addresses questions such as:

- What can we learn from the government's difficulties over ID cards and 42-day pre-charge detention for terrorist suspects?
- What did the new National Security Strategy consist of?
- Why was this new strategy considered necessary in 2008?
- Has the government struck the right balance between the demands of security and the need to protect individual liberties?

What can we learn from the government's difficulties over ID cards and 42-day pre-charge detention for terrorist suspects?

ID cards

The ID card scheme had faced opposition at Westminster from the outset. Although there was broad public support for the measure, at least early on, a growing number of politicians, irrespective of party ties, argued against a measure that they regarded as being at best of little benefit and at worst a blight on individual liberties.

By 2008, the campaign against the scheme had crystallised around four main arguments:
- that the introduction of such cards would allow the government to track and monitor the movement and perhaps ultimately the general behaviour of all citizens in a manner that threatened fundamental civil liberties
- that the technology simply would not work in the desired manner
- that government agencies could not be trusted to store the relevant data securely

- that the supposed benefits of the scheme did not justify the cost, either to the state or to those applying for cards

Although the first two arguments had been present from the earliest stages of the debate over ID cards, it was the third and fourth points that came to the fore in 2008. The issue of data security was certainly at the heart of growing opposition to the scheme. With the Home Office and a number of other government departments guilty of serious losses of sensitive personal data between 2005 and 2008, some questioned whether any agency could be trusted with the kind of biometric data that the government was intending to hold under the scheme. While such risks might be acceptable if the scheme were voluntary — as citizens could weight the convenience of having a biometric card against the risk of their data being lost — the same would not be true if all citizens were required to apply for one of the new cards. As David Davis noted in the *Guardian* on 7 March 2008, 'the Home Secretary's claim that she is offering people a choice is misleading — identity cards will still be compulsory. The government has lost the argument. They have lost 25 million personal records. And they have lost the public's trust'.

The spiralling costs of the proposed ID card scheme also provoked criticism. The Liberal Democrats were quick to promise that they would scrap the scheme, both on principle and on cost: the party planned to use some of the money saved to fulfil its pledge of tax cuts for low and middle income earners. The estimated cost to the individual of applying for the cards offered under the scheme also became a major issue as the fine detail started to trickle out. Although polls in 2008 showed that the majority of the public still believed that cards would be free, the projected cost had in fact risen to over £30 for the standard card and £93 for the combined ID card and passport.

The home secretary, Jacqui Smith, had initially hoped to push ahead by fast-tracking cards for public sector workers, but it was clear by the end of 2008 that little progress would be made ahead of the next general election.

The battle over 42-day detention
Brown's determination to extend the upper limit for pre-trial detention of terrorist suspects from 28 days to 42 days — a number widely seen as having simply been plucked out of thin air — appeared doomed by the summer of 2008.

Opposition to extending pre-trial detention
- The original plan for 90-day pre-charge detention had resulted in Tony Blair's only Commons defeat as prime minister back in 2005.
- The 28-day limit salvaged from that defeat had only been used on a handful of occasions since 2006. Indeed, it was reported that no one had been held for more than 14 days pre-charge in the 9 months to 23 April 2008.
- The report of the Home Affairs Select Committee found no justification for extending the existing 28-day limit.

- The head of MI5, Jonathan Evans, offered no evidence in support of extending the limit: his predecessor, Lady Manningham-Buller, used her maiden Lords speech on 8 July to oppose a higher upper limit, both on principle and on practicalities.
- The Director of Public Prosecutions (DPP), Sir Ken Macdonald, argued against such a change on the grounds that it was unnecessary (see Box 4.1).
- The Council of Europe's Human Rights Commissioner, Thomas Hammarberg, called the plan 'excessive and counterproductive', arguing that it was out of line with rules in other European countries.
- Senior police officers made public their fears that the measure could cause friction between the police and the Muslim community, create pressure on officers to find or even manufacture evidence, and damage the police's reputation among ethnic minority communities.

Box 4.1   The DPP's line

'For our part as prosecutors, we don't perceive any need for the period of 28 days to be increased. Our experience has been that we have managed comfortably within 28 days. We have therefore not asked for an increase in 28 days. It is possible to set up all sorts of hypotheses...Anything is possible — the question is whether it's remotely likely.'

Source: quoted in the *Guardian*, 23 April 2008.

The Commons battle — a Pyrrhic victory?

With the final Commons vote on the measure scheduled for 11 June and a second major Commons defeat for New Labour looking almost inevitable, government ministers went into overdrive. The then Home Office minister, Tony McNulty, moved to reassure backbench MPs by suggesting that the new upper limit would be utilised in the rarest of circumstances. The home secretary, Jacqui Smith, went further, offering a raft of concessions including a promise of a parliamentary debate within 7–10 days of such powers being invoked and a guarantee that, once in play, such powers would be subject to review every 30 days.

Significant pressure was also being applied behind the scenes. The Labour chair of the Home Affairs Select Committee — one-time minister for Europe, Keith Vaz — distanced himself from his own committee's recommendations by making public his support for the measure on the eve of the Commons vote. The subsequent leaking of a letter addressed to Vaz from the government chief whip, Geoff Hoon (dated 12 June) — in which Hoon thanked him and said that he trusted Vaz would be 'appropriately rewarded' for his support — led to accusations that Vaz had been offered a knighthood in return for his backing. The suggestion that other potential opponents of the bill had been bought off with the offer of concessions in other areas of policy resulted in the Liberal Democrat leader Nick Clegg dubbing the government's 315–306 Commons victory as a 'victory for pork barrel politics'. The nine DUP MPs, in particular, were said to have traded their support in return for major concessions, including an extra £1.2 billion of funding for Ulster and a promise that the more liberal abortion laws operating in the rest of the UK would not be extended to the province. It was said that the support of other MPs was garnered through concessions ranging from enhanced compensation for miners to the lifting of sanctions on Cuba.

While such stories made good copy in the broadsheets, this was more theatre than real politics. Whereas government ministers were quick to hail their narrow victory on 11 June, it was apparent even at the time that, although the Commons battle had been won, the war over 42-day detention was far from over. Indeed, while some praised the then shadow home secretary David Davis's decision to resign and re-contest his Commons seat on the issue of civil liberties following the Commons vote, many questioned his timing: why make such a stand when the bill had not yet passed the Lords?

Defeat in the Lords
The widely anticipated Lords defeat on 13 October (309–118) and the government's immediate decision to remove the 42-day provision simply served to underline the pointlessness of Davis's grand gesture. It also fuelled broader unease regarding Labour's strategy. Many of those outside of government failed to grasp why it was that the Labour administration had remained so wedded to ideas that had provoked such an unfavourable reaction both on their own back benches and within Parliament as a whole. Although the broader public appeared to accept the need for such measures, in theory at least, the opposition at Westminster (particularly in the Lords) was always likely to cause the government unnecessary angst at a time when it was struggling on so many other fronts.

What did the new National Security Strategy consist of?

At face value, the National Security Strategy encapsulated all that A-level coursework moderators dread most, for this was a sprawling 64-page document low on originality and weak in form. Although it contained little that could be considered even remotely controversial, the document appeared more concerned with redefining and linking together existing threats and responses than with offering anything genuinely new. As Martin Kettle implied in the *Guardian* (see Box 4.2), it was tempting to write the whole thing off as a 'paper exercise'.

Box 4.2 What does it add up to?

Civil servants listening to Gordon Brown's announcement of the government's National Security Strategy must have felt a bit like Molière's Monsieur Jourdain — the man who discovered to his surprise that he had been speaking prose for

40 years without knowing it. According to the prime minister, the nature of the threats to national security has 'changed beyond recognition'. Today's threats come from international terrorism, crime, energy shortage, climate change and pandemics.

Judging by Brown's definition, the environment and health departments are now in the front line alongside the defence and home departments. The doctor who administers your vaccine is suddenly on a par with the police officer. Like Mr Jourdain, doctors will have to think of themselves in new ways.

Source: Martin Kettle, 'Threat fret', *Guardian*, 19 March 2008.

Aims and objectives

The new strategy (see Box 4.3) was rooted in the notion that some way should be found to link up the various national and international bodies charged with dealing with threats to the nation's security — whether human (e.g. terrorism) or environmental (e.g. extreme weather patterns, or disputes over dwindling resources).

Box 4.3 The rationale behind the strategy

The scope and approach of this strategy reflects the way our understanding of national security has changed. In the past, the state was the traditional focus of foreign, defence and security policies, and national security was understood as dealing with the protection of the state and its vital interests from attacks by other states. Over recent decades, our view of national security has broadened to include threats to individual citizens and to our way of life, as well as to the integrity and interests of the state.

That is why this strategy deals with transnational crime, pandemics and flooding — not part of the traditional idea of national security, but clearly challenges that can affect large numbers of our citizens, and which demand some of the same responses as more traditional security threats, including terrorism. The broad scope of this strategy also reflects our commitment to focus on the underlying drivers of security and insecurity, rather than just immediate threats and risks.

Source: *The National Security Strategy of the United Kingdom: Security in an interdependent world* (Cm7291), 19 March 2008.

The anti-terrorist part of the document was built on an approach referred to simply as 'CONTEST' — the cross-governmental counter-terrorism strategy first advanced in 2006. CONTEST comprised four main themes:

- **pursue:** stopping terrorist attacks
- **protect:** strengthening our protection against attack
- **prepare:** mitigating the impact of attacks
- **prevent:** stopping people becoming terrorists or supporting violent extremism

This approach to countering terrorism recognised the need not only to coordinate the efforts of different government departments and agencies within the UK, but also to work at both intergovernmental and supranational level. A similar multi-tier approach to security issues was also present in the sections of the strategy that addressed the threats posed by serious organised crime and civil emergencies resulting from natural events such as floods and disease.

Although the new strategy document only offered a single concrete proposal — the suggestion that the UK might finally establish a US-style National Security Council — it did at least offer a clear rationale: its desire to see all threats to UK security, whether internal or external, human or environmental, treated equally seriously.

Why was this new strategy considered necessary in 2008?

The 2008 strategy document was born of a desire to coordinate the often disparate and sometimes contradictory efforts of various UK bodies, their foreign counterparts and supranational organisations. Although the UK government had established a number of new agencies, passed numerous pieces of legislation, and spent enormous sums of money in the wake of 9/11 (see Box 4.4), there was a sense that much of the policy had been 'reactive' as opposed to 'proactive'. The new strategy sought to make the necessary connections between different aspects of UK security and put in place the means by which responses could be properly coordinated across different levels of government.

Box 4.4 **Maintaining national security in the wake of 9/11**

Strategy

- 2002: New Strategic Defence Review Chapter sets out the contribution of the armed forces to counter-terrorism.
- 2006: The first cross-government counter-terrorism strategy, CONTEST, and cross-government counter-proliferation framework.
- 2008: New Foreign and Commonwealth Office (FCO) strategic framework underlines how national security depends on cooperation with other nations.

Structures

- 2001: Conflict Prevention Pools to improve joint working between the FCO, the Ministry of Defence, and the Department for International Development; and new Cabinet Office structures dealing with emergencies.
- 2003: Joint Terrorism Analysis Centre bringing together expertise from the police, intelligence agencies and 16 departments.
- 2006: Serious and Organised Crime Agency established.
- 2007: Office for Security and Counter-Terrorism established to manage the cross-government counter-terrorism effort; new UK Border Agency announced; and new Cabinet Committee on National Security, International Relations and Development, bringing together ministers from across government.

Resources

- Counter-terrorism and intelligence funding increased from £1 billion (2001) to £2.5 billion (2008). Projected at £3.5 billion for 2010/11.
- A new Single Security and Intelligence Budget operating across different departments and agencies.
- The longest period of sustained real growth in the defence budget since the 1980s, as well as increased spending on dealing with global conflict.

Legislation

- New powers to tackle terrorism and secure successful prosecutions, including: control orders; extended stop and search powers; new offences of acts preparing, encouraging and glorifying terrorism, and training for terrorism; extended pre-charge detention; and extended proscription of terrorist organisations.
- New powers for both central and local government to coordinate responses to domestic emergencies.

Source: *The National Security Strategy of the United Kingdom: Security in an interdependent world* (Cm7291), 19 March 2008.

This, it was argued, would make a good deal of sense in a world where those engaged in commissioning acts of terrorism, those involved in serious organised crime, and those who stood to benefit from conflict resulting from scarcity of resources and market instability, were increasingly one and the same.

Has the government struck the right balance between the demands of security and the need to protect individual liberties?

Although the government's 2008 strategy document was concerned with bringing greater coherence and coordination to the various elements of security policy developed over the last decade, many questioned whether such policies had in themselves crossed a certain line.

Among the most vocal of critics was journalist Henry Porter, whose reprise of the oral evidence he had delivered to Parliament's Joint Committee on Human Rights was published in the *Observer* on 3 March 2008 (see Box 4.5). Porter's study gave a stark illustration of the sheer range and volume of measures enacted by the government in recent years. It is only when one digs below the surface of this summary, however, that the true extent of many of the powers granted to public officials since 2001 becomes apparent.

Box 4.5 How the government has undermined society

Communications

- Under the Regulation of Investigatory Powers Act (2002), government agencies make 500,000 secret interceptions of email, internet connections and standard mail.

- Since summer 2007, the government and some 700 agencies have had access to all landline and mobile phone records.

Databases

- Police build a network of Automatic Number Plate Recognition (ANPR) cameras on motorways and in town centres. Data stored for 2 years.
- The National Identity Register will store details of every verification made by ID-card holders. Data used without knowledge of citizens. ID-card enrolment will require biometric details and large amounts of personal data.
- Home Office plans to take 19 pieces of information from anyone travelling abroad. No statutory basis.

Free expression

- Public order laws have been used to curtail free expression.
- The Race and Religious Hatred Act (2006) bans incitement of hatred on religious grounds.
- Terror laws are used to ban freedom of expression in some areas.

The courts

- ASBO legislation introduces hearsay evidence which can result in jail sentence.
- The Criminal Justice Act (2003) attacks jury trial.
- Admissibility of bad character evidence, previous convictions and acquittals.
- The Proceeds of Crime Act (2002) allows confiscation of assets without prosecution.
- Special Immigration Appeals Court hearings held in secret.

Terror laws

- Terror laws used to stop and search. Current rate is 50,000 per annum.
- A maximum of 28 days' detention without charge.

Source: Henry Porter, 'Why I told Parliament: you've failed us on liberty', *Observer*, 3 March 2008.

Surveillance society

The very first measure listed by Porter, the Regulation of Investigatory Powers Act (2002), has been applied in ways in which those drafting the original bill must surely never have intended. On 14 May, in an article entitled 'Council used terror law to spy on fisherman', the *Guardian* reported that Poole Borough Council had used the Act — originally intended for use against terrorism and cyber-crime — to monitor fishermen suspected of damaging Dorset's shellfish populations. The council, which admitted to using the Act on 17 occasions since 2005, had previously used the same powers to spy on a family in order to ensure that they were resident within their declared school catchment area. Other councils, it was reported, had used the powers to undertake covert surveillance on rogue traders, alleged benefit cheats and those suspected of anti-social behaviour.

This is only one small part of the emergence of what some have called a surveillance society or CCTV nation. The UK now has more CCTV cameras than any

other country in Europe, with an estimated total of 4.2 million devices in use: one for every 14 residents. Indeed, it is said that one in five CCTV devices worldwide is located in the UK. Police use of secret recording equipment, phone taps and internet monitoring has also become more widespread. The revelation in 2008 that a conversation between Sadiq Khan MP and prison inmate Babar Ahmad had been recorded with the aid of a device concealed under a table at Woodhill Prison 2 years earlier appeared to challenge the convention that discussions between an MP and their constituents should be confidential. The fact that the two men had reportedly been discussing possible civil action against the police in respect of Ahmad's original arrest merely fuelled concerns regarding the potential abuse of such powers.

Far from reviewing the efficacy of such techniques in the wake of these and other revelations, 2008 saw the government looking to loosen further the regulations governing the use of phone taps and covert video or listening devices. However, there was little to suggest that a Conservative government would offer anything but more of the same. On 12 August, the *Guardian* reported that shadow home secretary Dominic Grieve — the man who had stepped into the breach when David Davis embarked on his crusade in June — was promising a massive extension of surveillance powers. Although Grieve cautioned that councils should not use either their existing powers, or those he intended to grant them, in order to pursue those engaged in trivial offences such as dog fouling, it was hard to see how the introduction of such blanket powers would result in anything less.

Seizure of personal assets

Although the Treasury's ability to freeze personal assets was based on a measure designed to target those suspected of giving financial aid to al-Qaeda and the Taliban, it has been applied far more widely. In a landmark ruling in April 2008, the High Court ruled that five men whose assets had been frozen by the Treasury, in spite of the fact that they had been convicted of no crime, had been treated unlawfully. In all, around £500,000 is said to have been frozen since the powers came into force in 2006 — with 70 individuals directly affected. At the height of the banking crisis in the autumn of 2008, it was even reported that the prime minister had used such anti-terrorist powers to freeze the UK assets of a number of Icelandic companies.

Curfews and the extension of police 'stop and search' powers

Putting the anti-terror measures to one side, there has also been criticism of the way in which other powers granted to the police over the last decade have been applied. July 2008 saw police in Redruth, Cornwall, launching 'Operation Goodnight' — a curfew scheme for unsupervised children (9 p.m. for under-15s and 8 p.m. for under-10s). Although this measure, introduced under powers granted in the Anti-social Behaviour Act (2003), was said to be voluntary, all unsupervised children on the streets after-hours were to be routinely stopped and questioned.

The issue of how the police apply their powers to stop and search citizens has also provoked considerable debate. Although Henry Porter stated that the stop and search powers granted under anti-terror legislation had been used on just 50,000 occasions, reports in July suggested that the police had used their routine stop and search powers on a total of 955,000 instances in the year 2006–07 and had used the lesser power to stop and ask people to account for themselves on nearly 2 million occasions — a figure that was unlikely to have fallen in 2007–08 with stop and search being used extensively in response to the rise in youth knife crime.

Quasi-policing

Allied to the extension of police stop and search powers has been the rise in the number of Community Support Officers and the granting of extensive powers to stop and question citizens to many other local council employees. Both developments have been packaged as a way of freeing up police officers to tackle more serious offences, but many have regarded such schemes as a step on the road to some kind of Orwellian 'Big Brother state', particularly when taken alongside initiatives that encourage citizens to 'shop' their neighbours for offences as trivial as failing to sort their refuse properly.

Conclusions

It is inevitable, perhaps, that citizens will defer to government in times of national emergency: accepting restrictions on their civil liberties that they would surely never countenance in the normal course of events. Once passed into law, however, it is largely up to the authorities to determine precisely how such powers are applied and when (if ever) they are rescinded (see Box 4.6). The first-century Roman poet Decimus Junius Juvenal encapsulated this paradox when posing the question *'quis custodiet ipsos custodes?'* ('who is to guard the guards themselves?') As US cryptographer and computer expert Bruce Schneier remarked in Henry Porter's *Observer* article, 'It is poor civic hygiene to install technologies that could some day facilitate a police state'.

Box 4.6	Beware the new security state

The outgoing Director of Public Prosecutions, Sir Ken Macdonald QC, warned against 'the paraphernalia of paranoia' and 'medieval delusions'.

'We need to understand that it is in the nature of state power that decisions taken...[now] are likely to be with us for ever', 'and will in turn be built upon', he said in response to the Home Secretary's proposal for a new database of mobile and internet traffic.

'We should take great care to imagine the world we are creating before we build it,' he added, '[lest] we end up living with something we can't bear.'

Source: 'Prosecutor's security state fears', www.bbc.co.uk, 20 October 2008.

Summary

- Although the government failed to make significant progress either on its ID-card scheme or on the plan to extend the limit for the pre-charge detention of terrorist suspects to 42 days, 2008 did see the publication of a new National Security Strategy.

- This strategy put natural challenges — such as those posed by climate change, floods and pandemic disease — on a par with more traditional security threats such as terrorism.

- The new strategy sought to better coordinate the efforts of those national and international bodies charged with ensuring UK security.

- Although many welcomed this more holistic approach to security, some saw it largely as a 'paper exercise' — an initiative that offered little new in terms of hard policy.

- 2008 saw several commentators questioning the way in which many of those measures enacted since 9/11 had been applied by the police, local authorities and government agencies.

- Some argued that the relentless quest for ever greater security was being pursued at the expense of individual liberties; that the UK was fast becoming a 'national security state'.

Chapter 5

Nick Clegg: new beginning or more of the same?

Context

Nick Clegg became the leader of the Liberal Democrats on 18 December 2007, in the wake of a contest that had proven a good deal closer than many had anticipated. Whereas those picking up the reins from an unpopular or weak predecessor often enjoy a lengthy honeymoon period, Clegg had the misfortune of following on from Vince Cable, the man who had acted as caretaker leader following Menzies Campbell's resignation back in October 2007. Although few outside of the Westminster village had expected a great deal from Cable, his interim leadership had in fact proved remarkably successful, so much so that many questioned whether the party needed another leader at all.

This chapter examines Nick Clegg's first year as leader of the Liberal Democrats. In so doing it will address questions such as:

- How successfully was Clegg able to stamp his own personality on the party?
- Has Clegg's leadership brought about a significant shift in the party's outlook or policies?
- How has the party fared electorally under Clegg's leadership?
- Are the Liberal Democrats any closer to being elected to government now than they were a year ago?

How successfully was Clegg able to stamp his own personality on the party?

It would be fair to say that Nick Clegg's accession as leader of the Liberal Democrats came neither at a time nor in a style entirely of his own choosing. Whereas the former Eurocrat and MEP had been touted as a future party leader — a 'Liberal Democrat Cameron' — since he entered the Commons in 2005, little from that point on had gone entirely to plan.

Clegg had backed Menzies Campbell's successful leadership bid in January 2006, yet many regarded his support as tactical, in part at least. Campbell was, it was argued, a necessary expedient; a safe pair of hands following Charles Kennedy's forced resignation. The expectation was that the sexagenarian would step aside well ahead of the next general election, thus making way for a younger, more 'dynamic' candidate. Chris Huhne and Simon Hughes, Campbell's chief opponents in 2006, may well have considered

themselves experienced enough to negate the need for such an interim leadership, but Clegg had been an MP for just 8 months at the time of Kennedy's resignation.

Although it was no surprise, therefore, that September 2007 saw Clegg going public with his desire to run for the leadership of the party in the event that Campbell stood down from his post, his willingness to offer himself up long before any vacancy existed did not play well with party loyalists. This left Clegg in a difficult position when Campbell unexpectedly stood down on 15 October. Criticisms of Clegg's supposed disloyalty played into the hands of his chief rival for the leadership, Chris Huhne, who had remained loyal to Campbell throughout. The result was that, far from being the walkover for Clegg that many had predicted, the battle for the Liberal Democrat leadership was ultimately the closest race on record — with Clegg only securing a 511-vote winning margin.

The modest scale of Clegg's winning margin and the sparkling performances of the acting leader Vince Cable at PMQs did little to unite the party behind their new leader. Indeed, some went as far as to question whether Clegg should have won at all (see Box 5.1).

Box 5.1 The real Liberal Democrat leader?

According to one account of the leadership contest last December, Chris Huhne would be the Liberal Democrat chief were it not for hundreds of ballot papers being held up by the Christmas post.

As many as 1,300 postal votes arrived after the deadline of 15 December and an unofficial check of the papers showed that Mr Huhne had enough of a majority among them to hand him victory.

Thousands of members had decided to leave it late in order to see how the contest between the two men developed. A rogue briefing document from the Huhne camp describing his rival as 'Calamity Clegg' may have contributed to the late surge for their man.

Source: *Independent on Sunday*, 6 April 2008.

Despite his narrow margin of victory, Clegg wasted little time in setting the party on a new path (see Box 5.2). Although his impromptu admission on BBC Radio 5 Live that he did not believe in God certainly helped to establish Clegg as a leader who was not afraid to give a straight answer to a straight question (see Table 5.1), it marked the start of a difficult first few months in the hot seat for the member for Sheffield Hallam.

With Clegg's later admission that he had engaged in sex with 'not more than 30 women' earning him the moniker 'Cleggover', many in the media concurred with the *Independent*'s appraisal of his first 100 days as 'lacklustre'.

	Clegg	Brown	Cameron
Strong, *or*	23	29	57
Weak	50	67	33
Winner, *or*	21	21	60
Loser	56	74	31
Up to the job of being prime minister, *or*	18	25	55
Not up to the job	59	72	37
In touch, *or*	37	27	56
Out of touch	42	71	37
Means what he says, *or*	30	31	30
Says what he thinks people want to hear	51	66	63
For the many, *or*	43	41	52
For the few	39	54	40

Source: from a Populus poll for *The Times*, 8 July 2008.

Table 5.1 Leaders' images (%)

The leader's approval rating (calculated by subtracting the percentage who disapprove of one's leadership from those who approve) had fallen to a low of −6 points by the start of April. Thereafter, however, things picked up markedly. In May and June he recorded +7 and +6 point scores respectively, and by September, just ahead of his first party conference as leader, he had reached the dizzy heights of +8 points. Although such an impressive headline figure disguised the fact that 44% of those questioned still fell into the 'don't know' category (see Table 5.2), this was nonetheless a considerable transformation. More impressive still was the fact that the turnaround in the Liberal Democrat leader's fortunes had come not as a result of his machinations on the existence of God or in recognition of his sexual prowess, but instead in the wake of a series of policy initiatives that challenged popular preconceptions regarding his party and, for a time at least, put both Labour and the Conservatives on the back foot.

	Clegg	Brown	Cameron
General public (18+)			
Satisfied	32	24	48
Dissatisfied	24	69	32
Don't know	44	7	20
Index (+/−)	+8	−45	+16
Party supporters only			
Satisfied	60	51	79
Dissatisfied	23	43	12
Don't know	17	6	9
Index (+/−)	+37	+8	+67

Source: data from Ipsos MORI September Political Monitor (2008).

Table 5.2 Satisfaction with prime minister/party leader

Has Clegg's leadership brought about a significant shift in the party's outlook or policies?

Testing the water?

Despite some difficult headlines for Clegg early on in the year, his first few months as leader saw him trailing some innovative policy proposals. In January he was suggesting that a Liberal Democrat government might take all schools out of state control and make it easier for parents and others in the community to set up new institutions. Later in the same month, he promised a further £2 billion to help cover the cost of providing care for the elderly, while acknowledging that the Scottish programme offering free nursing care for all could not be extended south of the border.

February was just as busy for Clegg. First came a preview of the Liberal Democrats' plans for the National Health Service, with the announcement that those waiting for treatment for mental health problems would have to wait no longer than 13 weeks for a consultation. Lamenting the UK's emergence as a 'Prozac nation', Clegg called for an end to the ever-growing numbers of people in receipt of prescriptions for anti-depressants.

February also saw Clegg appointing Jeremy Browne as the Liberal Democrats' Treasury no. 2 and charging him with the task of finding the 3% cuts in departmental budgets necessary to deliver the £20 billion earmarked for new Liberal Democrat initiatives. The month closed with Clegg calling for a new referendum on whether or not the UK should remain in the European Union, the first since 1975. This was, Clegg maintained, a way of ending the damaging debate over Europe (see Box 5.3). The move was also aimed at diffusing intra-party divisions ahead of the vote on whether or not there should be a referendum on the Lisbon Treaty; although Clegg's insistence that Liberal Democrats abstained on the Commons vote still precipitated the resignation of three members of his frontbench team.

Box 5.3 **Clegg's call for a referendum on EU membership**

The debate about Europe has been a thorn in the side of British politics for decades...If you're pro-European, as I am, you're accused of being a sell-out. If you're anti-European, like most Conservatives, you're accused of being a head-banger. It isn't new, but it isn't edifying either. It's time...for a debate politicians have been too cowardly to hold for 30 years – time for a referendum on the big question. Do we want to be in or out? Nobody in Britain under the age of 51 has ever been asked that simple question. None of them were eligible to vote in that 1975 referendum. That includes half of all MPs. Two generations have never had their say.

Source: Nick Clegg, 'Ask the under-50s', *Guardian*, 25 February 2008.

With the Conservatives making ground in the polls and Labour struggling to find their stride, March saw Clegg setting out the Liberal Democrats' terms for entering into a coalition, in the event that the next general election should result in a hung parliament. The price, it was revealed on 10 March, would be a commitment to a constitutional convention charged with the task of drafting a new constitutional settlement for the UK. One element of such a settlement had already been trailed on 6 March with the suggestion that the UK might adopt the recall system used in many US states, whereby elected politicians and officials who fail to discharge their duties in an appropriate manner can be removed by a publicly initiated popular vote.

Although Clegg had been relatively quiet on the topic of foreign affairs, the month of May saw the Liberal Democrat leader visiting Afghanistan in order to offer his party's support for the UK mission in Helmand. The Liberal Democrats had opposed the intervention in Iraq, but Clegg was keen to set out his view that the fight against the Taliban was central to the security of both the region and the UK itself. Two days later, on 20 May, Clegg was back in the UK addressing the centre-right think-tank Policy Exchange on the subject of his desire to shift the burden of taxation away from the UK's poorest citizens.

All of this served to enhance Clegg's credibility at a time when Labour appeared rudderless and the Conservatives remained unwilling to commit policies to

paper. However, it was the party's annual conference in Bournemouth that saw these threads of policy coalesce into a more coherent whole.

Establishing a programme for government

The annual conference, held in Bournemouth (13–17 September), saw Clegg in a combative mood. Many of the threads of policy identified earlier in the year were brought together in a provisional programme that challenged many of the tenets upon which the party had been based since its formation in 1988.

Repositioning the party on the issue of Europe

Of the big three UK parties, the Liberal Democrats have traditionally been the most enthusiastic supporters of the European project. Clegg himself had served as a leading official at the European Commission in the 1990s and was also an MEP for a time before he was elected to the Commons in 2005. It was a surprise to many, therefore, that the 2008 conference saw the Liberal Democrats abandoning their orthodox Europhile stance in favour of something rather more circumspect. As the party's Treasury spokesman, Vince Cable, put it, 'there are various things that we have learnt about Euroland, and about the Eurozone, which are clearly problems that need to be resolved...The Common Agricultural Policy is a complete disgrace...a lot of institutional reform is necessary' (*Observer*, 14 September).

Although Clegg had already indicated a more direct approach to tackling the European issue with his call for a referendum on continued UK membership back in February, the debate at the conference took things a stage further — offering the possibility that any area of policy that had traditionally undermined the party's attempts to reach out to a wider audience would be neutralised as an electoral issue.

Modifying the party's approach to taxation and government spending

The Liberal Democrats have long been associated with a commitment to increase public spending and have not been afraid, in the past, to make public their plans to fund such programmes through an increase in the basic rate of income tax. As Chris Huhne noted at the conference, however, there was a clear paradox in the fact that while government spending had increased by 46% in real terms since 1997, there was still widespread concern with both the range and the quality of services provided. It might be time, Huhne suggested, to try something different.

An indication of just how different the party's new position would be had been provided in February when Clegg instructed Jeremy Browne to find the savings across government departments necessary to deliver a £20 billion cut in spending. The true scale of what the Liberal Democrats were planning only became apparent, however, at the conference.

Having already pledged to cut the basic rate of income tax by 4p in the pound, the conference saw Clegg offering the prospect that this might be extended to

6p by using £4 billion of the savings identified by Browne and closing up some of the £5 billion worth of tax loopholes that, according to Cable, allowed higher earners to avoid paying taxes such as stamp duty. The remaining £16 billion in savings from existing spending (e.g. the shelving of the ID-card scheme) would be redistributed to fund the Liberal Democrats' ambitious plans in education and healthcare. Some £5 billion would fund the 'pupil premium', a scheme designed to channel additional funds to schools serving particularly deprived communities. The party would also abandon the National Curriculum, returning control of what is taught in schools to schools themselves. Further moneys would provide a new 'NHS guarantee', a promise that patients would be entitled to free private treatment if the NHS could not accommodate their medical needs within agreed time limits.

Although many were stunned by the sheer scale of the Liberal Democrats' proposed tax cuts — this at a time when even the Conservatives were unwilling to commit to a significant reduction in the basic rate of tax — Clegg defended the move, as reported in the *Guardian* on 13 September: 'Aspiring to hand back money to people from central government', he maintained, 'is impeccably liberal.' The programme also proved controversial at the conference, but the party moved to approve the plans as set out in Clegg's 'Make it Happen' document.

Moving towards a more realistic foreign policy
The party conference called for a full review of long-term strategic defence planning with a view to developing a foreign policy more clearly linked to available resources. Although Clegg's commitment to the mission in Afghanistan remained (see above), it was suggested that the conventional military resources needed in such theatres of war could be funded by a 50% cut in the UK's nuclear arsenal and a further delay in the decision over the replacement of Trident.

Clegg in the spotlight
Clegg's keynote conference speech looked to reach out to disaffected Tory and Labour voters. Characterising Brown's administration as 'a zombie government, a cross between *Shaun of the Dead* and *I'm Sorry I Haven't a Clue*', Clegg's 38-minute speech was well received both within party ranks and among those in the media and the broader public. Most, if not all, were even prepared to overlook his gaffe in saying that the state pension was just £30 per week when it is in fact three times that figure.

How has the party fared electorally under Clegg's leadership?

It had been the sight of the Liberal Democrats sliding towards their lowest ever showing in the polls that had prompted Menzies Campbell's departure and — ultimately — the confirmation of Clegg's election as leader on 18 December. That descent had eventually bottomed out on 26 October with a

YouGov *Daily Telegraph* poll showing that the party had the support of just 11% of voters. It was obvious, therefore, that the Liberal Democrats' poll results and election performance under Clegg would be the focus of considerable interest.

Overall, it is probably fair to say that the party performed a little better — certainly no worse — under Clegg than it had in the year before his accession. As well as the gradual improvement in his own approval rating over the course of his first year, the party as a whole gained some encouragement from an ICM voting intentions survey on September 2008, which gave the party the support of around 17% of those expressing a preference — broadly in line with the kinds of figures the party had achieved before at similar stages in the electoral cycle.

When one includes the data for those who 'Would not vote', 'Don't know' or 'Refused' to respond in such polls, however, the picture is far less positive (see Table 5.3). In addition, although the detailed data showed that the movement of voters who had backed the party in 2005 towards Cameron's Conservatives had been arrested, these supporters had not returned their allegiance to the Liberal Democrats: they had instead joined the ranks of the 'Don't knows'. In short, although the party's slide in the polls had been halted, there was no immediate danger of the Liberal Democrats sweeping all before them in the event of a snap general election.

	August	**September**
Conservative	28	25
Labour	17	20
Liberal Democrat	12	10
SNP	2	2
Plaid Cymru	0	1
Green Party	1	1
UK Independence Party	1	0
Other	1	2
Would not vote	12	12
Don't know	17	20
Refused	8	8

Source: www.icmresearch.co.uk, August and September 2008.

Table 5.3 ICM voting intentions surveys (rounded)

The Liberal Democrats' performance in actual elections was — as outlined in Chapters 2 and 3 — somewhat mixed. The party performed relatively well in the local elections, making a net gain of one council and three councillors compared to its net loss of four councils and 246 councillors in May 2007. The elections to the London Assembly offered rather less encouragement, with the party securing only 3 of the 25 seats available (down 2 on 2004). Although the party's share of the vote also fell in the London mayoral election, this was far less damaging, as the nature of the contest and the system used meant that the Liberal Democrat vote was always likely to be squeezed.

The Liberal Democrat performance in the various by-elections held in 2008 was inconclusive. In some cases (e.g. Crewe and Glasgow East) the party's vote was squeezed amid tactical voting aimed at getting other parties (i.e. the Conservatives and the SNP) elected at Labour's expense. Henley, in contrast, saw the Liberal Democrats' second-place share of the vote increase as the Labour vote collapsed spectacularly. Both the Liberal Democrats and Labour decided against contesting Haltemprice and Howden, the by-election prompted by David Davis's decision to stand down and re-contest his seat over the issue of 42-day detention.

Conclusions: are the Liberal Democrats any closer to being elected to government now than they were a year ago?

Although Nick Clegg's suggestion that the Liberal Democrats were on course for government (see Box 5.4) resulted in him being branded a fantasist by some in the press, it was widely accepted that his first year in post had been a qualified success.

Box 5.4 **Nick Clegg's call to arms**

Nick Clegg yesterday echoed the words spoken in 1981 by David Steel, when he was Liberal leader, telling party members to 'go back to your constituencies and prepare for government'. Mr Clegg said, 'I can't tell you every step on the road for us...I can tell you where we're headed. Government.'

Source: 'Nick Clegg promises to banish horror of "zombie" Labour', *The Times*, 18 September 2008.

While it was true that the party often appeared at risk of being steered off-course by Clegg's candour during his first few months at the helm, the autumn conference saw the party establishing an imaginative and, some judged, more attractive programme of policies. Despite the headlines the day after his keynote speech, a more careful reading of Clegg's words reveals a leader clever enough to see that the Liberal Democrats cannot hope to be in government following the next general election — unless as a minor partner in a coalition. His assessment that his party was on the right road to take power — albeit at some point as yet unknown — was equally hard to dismiss entirely.

Summary

- The start of Nick Clegg's tenure as Liberal Democrat leader followed a period in which the party had struggled to make an impression in opinion polls, sliding to all-time low of just 11% in October 2007.

- The narrow margin of Clegg's victory in the leadership contest — and question marks over his performance in post during his first 100 days — led some to question whether they had chosen the right man for the job.

- By April 2008 the Liberal Democrats appeared to have turned the corner. Clegg's personal approval ratings had improved markedly and the party itself was also faring better in the polls.

- In terms of electoral performance, however, 2008 was a mixed year for the Liberal Democrats — although the local election results in May offered some encouragement.

- Under Clegg's leadership the Liberal Democrats adopted a range of policies that went against many of the things that the party had come to stand for in the two decades since it was formed.

- Clegg committed the party to significant cuts in the basic rate of income tax, a more cautious approach to relations with the EU, and a marked shift in government spending priorities.

- The party closed its annual conference in Bournemouth in an optimistic mood on 17 September.

Chapter 6

Pressure groups: the return of the big beasts?

Context

17 February 2008 marked the 50th anniversary of the meeting at Westminster Central Hall that had launched the Campaign for Nuclear Disarmament (CND). At that inaugural event, luminaries such as Bertrand Russell, J. B. Priestley and Michael Foot had addressed a crowd of some 5,000 individuals. In its heyday in the 1960s, the CND and its iconic white-on-black symbol were at the forefront of UK pressure group activity. Yet the passing of its half-centenary might easily have gone unreported in an age in which smaller, single-issue groups and more spontaneous protest movements and marches have eclipsed the mass membership groups once so central to any study of UK pressure group politics.

This chapter examines the apparent resurgence of a number of mass membership organisations — the 'big beasts' of the pressure group landscape — in recent months. In so doing it will address questions such as:

- Did 2008 witness a change in the nature, scale and scope of environmental protest?
- Why were trade unions experiencing something of a renaissance in 2008?
- Does CND still serve a useful purpose, 50 years on?

Did 2008 witness a change in the nature, scale and scope of environmental protest?

Environmental pressure groups such as Greenpeace enjoyed more extensive and — on the whole — more favourable media coverage in 2008.

In February, four Greenpeace protesters were pictured perched atop a BA Airbus A320 at Heathrow, unfurling a banner declaring, 'Climate Emergency. No 3rd Runway'. In September, six other Greenpeace activists were cleared of causing £30,000 worth of damage to a 200-metre chimney at the coal-fired Kingsnorth power station in Kent in October 2007. The group's defence, that the immediate risk posed by climate change necessitated their action, was not dissimilar to that used successfully by other activists in recent years (see Box 6.1), with the growing belief that unchecked emissions might take the world beyond a global warming 'tipping point' only serving to swell the ranks of those prepared to run the risk of a day in court.

Chapter **6**

Box 6.1 Eco-warriors cleared

2008 Six Greenpeace activists were cleared of causing £30,000 of damage to a chimney at Kingsnorth power station in Kent.

2000 A Norwich jury found the Greenpeace director Lord Melchett and 27 activists not guilty of causing criminal damage to a field of genetically modified (GM) crops.

2000 Five Greenpeace volunteers were found not guilty of criminal damage after occupying an incinerator.

1999 Three women were cleared of causing £80,000 damage to a Trident nuclear submarine's computer equipment.

1996 A Liverpool jury acquitted four women who caused £1.5 million damage to a Hawk fighter jet at a British Aerospace factory.

Source: J. Vidal, 'Not guilty: the Greenpeace activists who used climate change as a legal defence', *Guardian*, 11 September 2008.

Although it is tempting to see such events as evidence of a sharp upturn in Greenpeace's fortunes, the situation is, in fact, rather more complex. Greenpeace's activities in support of both causes were neither conceived nor executed entirely alone, but as part of a more coordinated effort involving a number of other pressure groups. For example, the Greenpeace protest at Heathrow on 25 February was followed by a second stunt 2 days later. The latter saw Tamsin Omond, an activist from the protest group Plane Stupid (see Box 6.2), take to the roof of the Palace of Westminster in order to launch paper aeroplanes made from documents condemning the government's plans for a third runway at Heathrow, and unfurl two massive banners: one demanding 'No third runway', the other labelling Parliament as 'British Airports Authority HQ'.

Box 6.2 After 'Swampy'

A decade after Swampy defied Britain's road-building programme and invested the eco-protester as national celebrity, a new wave of campaigners is forming around the issue of air travel and global warming.

The umbrella group Plane Stupid was founded 3 years ago by university graduates Richard George (27), Graham Thompson (34) and Joss Garman (22), as the anti-Iraq war movement petered out in resentment that million-strong protest marches had not changed the government's mind. 'What we saw with the roads protests,' Garman said, 'was that people were digging tunnels and attaching themselves to diggers because they realised too late what was going on. We are better prepared now. The stakes are so high this time.'

Source: D. Milmo and O. Bowcott, 'New wave protesters target airport expansion', *Guardian*, 1 March 2008.

The alleged crime for which the 'Greenpeace six' were acquitted in September 2008 should also be seen in its broader context. It was the proposed construction of the first new coal-fired power station in the UK for 30 years, at the same Kingsnorth site, that provided the focus for the week-long climate camp protests in July (see www.climatecamp.org.uk). These protests were in turn linked to the earlier protests at Heathrow, with the climate camp protesters having gathered at the airport before marching to Kingsnorth.

In truth, therefore, the events of 2008 should be seen not as a return to an earlier age of pressure group activity, but as part of a process by which the activities of a range of like-minded groups are becoming more coordinated: something akin to the kind of 'joined-up', 'umbrella group' activity seen in earlier campaigns against the poll tax (1990), the war in Iraq (2003) and world poverty (2005). The year 2008 therefore marked the point at which the traditional stalwarts of the environmental movement united with a new generation of activists who had learned their lessons from the anti-road protests of the 1990s.

Why were trade unions experiencing something of a renaissance in 2008?

In much the same way that environmental pressure groups appeared to have come of age in 2008, trade unions were also staging something of a fightback. Many felt that Labour's return to office in 1997 would herald a sea change in the fortunes of trade unions. In reality, however, the nature of the economy, the dynamics of the labour market and Labour's unwillingness to reverse the anti-union legislation of the 1980s meant that there was only limited change in the short term (Box 6.3).

In spite of this lack of progress, the main unions nonetheless appeared unwilling to rock the boat following Labour's 18 years in opposition. The party's willingness to embrace the European Social Chapter, the introduction of the minimum wage and the launch of the tax credits scheme also served to reassure those union officials who may have hoped for a return to the days of 'beer and sandwiches at No. 10'. As long as New Labour fared well in the opinion polls and at the ballot box, therefore, most unions appeared reluctant to criticise the government publicly.

> ### Box 6.3 **Unions in crisis?**
>
> - Although the workforce has grown by over 2 million since 1997, union membership has been stuck at around 7 million.
> - The challenge of union growth is particularly difficult in the private sector, where only one in five workers are now union members.
> - An ongoing series of mergers will result in fewer but larger unions.
> - Unions need to move the focus away from pay disputes and industrial action towards providing advice on pensions and training opportunities, and offering guidance on how to find a better work–life balance.
>
> Source: from an article by Ian McCartney, Labour Party chair, April 2005.

By 2008, however, things had changed markedly:

- New Labour's first decade in office had witnessed a widening of the gulf between the richest and the poorest UK citizens.
- Public sector pay deals had failed to keep pace with inflation.
- Poor poll ratings and disappointing results in by-elections and local elections meant that there was no longer a compelling reason for unions to moderate their criticism of the New Labour project.
- Labour's cash-flow problems made the party more reliant on union contributions than it had been at any time since the early 1990s.

The final factor had emerged as a major issue by the summer of 2008. The scandal over donations to the party and the subsequent police investigation into the alleged sale of peerages had served to scare off wealthy individual donors. As a result, the unions had once again become the chief source of Labour Party funding (see Box 6.4).

> ### Box 6.4 **Labour's cash crisis and the unions**
>
> Trade union leaders are to put a broad set of demands to Labour ahead of its next general election manifesto, including free school meals for all primary children and new flexible working rights for parents.
>
> Labour's financial crisis has put the unions in a powerful position. The party's accounts were only signed off after union leaders rallied to its financial support after a collapse in backing from wealthy donors.
>
> Source: P. Wintour and N. Watt, 'Unions put new demands to Brown', *Guardian*, 30 June 2008.

Why had the unions declined in the 1980s and 1990s?

The 1970s had been the decade of high union membership and militancy. The miners were widely credited with bringing down Edward Heath's Conservative government in 1974 and the 'Winter of Discontent' (1978–79) had precipitated the fall of James Callaghan's Labour administration.

All had changed by the late 1980s, however, as a result of three interconnected developments.

Changes in occupational structure

The collapse of the heavy and manufacturing industries led to the decline of the 'old working class' and the rise of a 'new working class' that was less cohesive, less militant and less heavily unionised (see Table 6.1).

Industry	% of workforce unionised
Top three	
Public administration and defence	57.3
Education	55.1
Electricity, gas and water supply	49.3
Bottom three	
Real estate and business services	10.0
Agriculture, forestry and fishing	9.0
Hotels and restaurants	5.6

Source: R Whitaker, 'In Focus: trade union membership', *Politics Review*, Vol.18, No.1 (2008).

Table 6.1 The scale of union membership

Anti-union legislation

A series of Acts passed in the 1980s (see Box 6.5) created a legal environment that was far less conducive to large-scale, coordinated union activity.

Box 6.5 **Thatcher and the unions**

The Trade Union Act (1984) and the Employment Acts of 1980, 1982, 1988 and 1989 had a massive cumulative effect on the ability of unions to act quickly and freely.

- Unions were no longer allowed to organise secondary or sympathy action or secondary or mass picketing.
- They were prevented from organising national strikes without gaining approval for action in each place of work through a secret ballot.
- A union had to organise secret ballots before strike action and could face sequestration — the freezing of its assets — if it engaged in illegal action.
- There was to be a trade union commissioner who would help finance court cases against unions.

The defeat of the National Union of Mineworkers in 1985 following a year-long strike marked a watershed in union power. The union that had brought down the Conservatives in the 1970s had in turn been brought down by the Conservatives in the 1980s.

Source: P. Fairclough (2006), *AS and A-Level Government and Politics*, Oxford University Press.

Labour Party reform

Labour's introduction of one member, one vote (OMOV) from 1993 saw the party move away from the power of the union 'block vote' at conferences. The reform of the method by which Labour leaders are elected also reduced union power, as did the party's success in attracting wealthy individual donors — because it allowed Labour to become less reliant on union funding.

Did 2008 witness a return to 1970s-style union power?

The simple answer to the question would be 'no'. Although strikes and other forms of industrial action were certainly on the increase in 2008, such activities still fell some way short of the levels experienced 30 years before (see Box 6.6).

Box 6.6 **A summer of discontent?**

The Conservatives' media allies are promoting fanciful comparisons with the turbulent 1970s. That claim is specious for a host of reasons, not least the battery of Thatcherite legal constraints that still curb union militancy.

Union membership is barely half its 1979 peak of 13.2 million. One million working days were lost to strike action in 2007, up 250,000 on 2006. That compares to 7.2 million in the 1980s (27.1 million for the miners' strike year of 1984) and the 1970s average of 12.9 million, which spiked at 29.5 million days in the real 'Winter of Discontent' that finished off Labour's last government in 1979.

Source: M. White, 'Union discontent, yes: but it's not the 1970s', *Guardian*, 26 June 2008.

While some conditions appeared more favourable to union activity in 2008, others remained largely unchanged:

- The massive changes that have taken place in the labour market since the 1970s are unlikely to be reversed.
- The disintegration of the old heavily unionised and more militant working class appears equally irreversible.
- Union membership remains some way short of the levels required to mount the kind of coordinated action needed to bring down a government (see Box 6.3 on p.54).
- The unions are still facing the dilemma that had first presented itself back in 1979: namely, whether there is any real benefit to be had from undermining a Labour administration when the most likely alternative — a Conservative government — might well be even less sympathetic to organised labour.

Does CND still serve a useful purpose, 50 years on?

CND's central ideal of unilateral nuclear disarmament proved untenable to many at a time when the Cold War was at its height and the UK's independent nuclear deterrent appeared to be so central to the nation's security. Indeed, it was in part the defence of unilateralism by Labour leader and CND leading light Michael Foot in the 1983 general election that led to the party's manifesto being described as 'the longest suicide note in history'. A decade on from that defeat, the collapse of the Soviet Union only appeared to vindicate those who had stood firm or taken a multilateralist approach to nuclear disarmament.

Although the debate over the UK's independent nuclear deterrent resurfaced in 2008 over precisely when (if not whether) to replace the Trident missile system, there was clear cross-party support for the construction of a new generation of nuclear reactors with a view to reducing the nation's carbon footprint.

While it is fair to say that groups such as Greenpeace and the trade unions appear to have adapted to the new political landscape, CND still appears wedded to aims and methods adopted in its infancy (see Box 6.7), and strangely out of step with the popular Zeitgeist. It is perhaps for these reasons that the coverage of its half-centenary anniversary was focused largely on the memories of those who had participated in the early Aldermaston marches, rather than on the group's current campaigns.

Box 6.7 **CND's stated objectives**

CND campaigns non-violently to rid the world of nuclear weapons and other weapons of mass destruction and to create genuine security for future generations. Our strategic objectives, as decided by delegates to our annual conference, are:

- elimination of British nuclear weapons and global abolition of nuclear weapons
- abolition of other threats of mass destruction or indiscriminate effect
- a nuclear-free, less militarised and more secure Europe
- the closure of the nuclear power industry

Source: www.cnduk.org, 12 November 2008.

Conclusions

A pressure group's success is commonly measured in terms of the extent to which it achieves its objectives. If we accept this broad definition, a group's chances of success will depend upon five key factors (see Box 6.8).

Box 6.8 **Five factors affecting group success**

- Group aims: 'achievability' and 'public receptivity'.
- Group specialism and expertise.
- Group status: whether it is an insider or an outsider.
- Group methodology: the strategy and tactics adopted by the group.
- Group resources: both human (e.g. size of membership, quality of membership) and financial.

Chief among these factors is group aims: the extent to which an individual group's ultimate objectives are practically achievable and whether or not such aims reflect the broader public sentiment.

It is this issue of 'public receptivity' that goes to the heart of why some of those groups identified in this chapter have fared so well in 2008, while others have laboured. While the CND chair, Kate Hudson, admitted that the group's aims were still regarded as 'a distant dream' by many, unions are clearly back in the public eye and environmental campaigners have seen their cause move centre-stage as a result of widespread concerns regarding climate change.

Summary

- The success of pressure groups is to a large degree predicated on their underlying aims and objectives, their methodologies and the prevailing political climate.
- The 1990s saw smaller, single-issue groups and protest movements proliferate, while larger, more conventional groups struggled to find traction.
- In 2008, however, larger groups such as Greenpeace and the trade unions experienced something of a renaissance as their respective causes found greater public sympathy.
- CND, in contrast, laboured in the year of its half-centenary in the face of broad political and popular support for the construction of a new generation of nuclear power stations. The goal of unilateral nuclear disarmament similarly appeared no closer than it had a generation before — perhaps even a little more distant.

Chapter 7

MPs' expenses: all aboard the gravy train?

Context

2008 saw the issue of MPs' pay and allowances coming under intense media scrutiny. Although such coverage was fuelled, in part, by the allegations surrounding the MP for Old Bexley and Sidcup, Derek Conway, it quickly descended into a more general debate over precisely how MPs were using (or perhaps abusing) their allowable expenses as a means of boosting their regular salary. In the media mêlée that ensued, all manner of hitherto unknown perks were laid bare, not least the so-called 'John Lewis list', from which, it was said, members could furnish their second homes at the taxpayers' expense.

This chapter examines the whole issue of MPs' pay and allowances. In so doing it will address questions such as:

- Why was Derek Conway singled out for such criticism in 2008?
- What is the additional costs allowance and why has it proven so controversial?
- Why didn't the Commons move more quickly to diffuse the situation?
- What can be done to restore confidence in the integrity of our MPs?

Why was Derek Conway singled out for such criticism in 2008?

On 30 January 2008, the Conservative MP for Old Bexley and Sidcup, Derek Conway, announced that he would not be contesting his seat at the next general election. By that stage Conway was not, in fact, a Conservative MP at all, the party whip having been withdrawn a day earlier as a result of the fallout from his alleged abuse of his MP's staffing allowance.

One of the most surprising features of the Conway scandal was the extent to which many fellow MPs appeared reluctant to criticise openly a colleague who had so obviously transgressed. The answer lies in the fact that Conway was not, in many respects, that unusual. While he claimed £140,916 in allowable expenses in 2006/07 on top of his £60,675 basic salary, others had received far more. The Labour MP for Dewsbury, Shahid Malik, for example, had racked up expenses of £185,421 in the same year and even Gordon Brown's cabinet ally Ed Balls had received £157,076. Indeed, according to the *Independent*, Balls and his wife, Yvette Cooper, had claimed a total of more than £307,000.

Conway's decision to use a large part of his £86,439 staffing allowance claim to employ members of his immediate family (see Table 7.1) was similarly unexceptional. In April 2008, the *Independent* published a list of 106 MPs who

employed at least one relative from their staffing allowances. Belfast East MP Peter Robinson, for example, had employed both his daughter (as office manager and private secretary) and his son (parliamentary assistant) using money from the £95,726 he had claimed for staffing in 2006/07.

Derek Conway MP	£60,675	Basic salary
	£21,177	Office costs
	£22,060	Second home allowance
	£3,936	Car allowance
	£86,439	Staff allowance
Colette Conway (wife)	£30,000	Per annum as a parliamentary assistant
Henry Conway (son)	£32,000	Over 3 years as a research assistant (18 hours a week)
Freddie Conway (son)	£45,163	Over 3 years as a research assistant (17 hours a week)

Source: *Guardian*, 30 January 2008.

Table 7.1 Keeping it in the family, the Conway way

In reality, it was not the scale or nature of Conway's claim that proved problematic, but his inability to provide sufficient evidence that his sons had done the kind of work that might have justified the payments. In the case of Conway's younger son, Freddie, the media coverage proved particularly damning, with revelations that the payments totalling £45,163 covered a 3-year period (2004–07) when he was enrolled on a full-time undergraduate course at Newcastle University.

Although there were few who would openly defend Conway's behaviour, the opacity of the regulations governing the accounting of payments made under the staffing allowance ensured that imposing a punishment on the Conservative MP was far harder than many had anticipated. While Conway's defence — that his behaviour was not uncommon and that he had not thought it necessary to keep a record of the work undertaken by his sons — was widely ridiculed, he was right in the sense that there had been no legal obligation for him to keep detailed records. Neither was Conway required at the time even to reveal publicly that he was employing his immediate family in this way (see Box 7.1).

While Conway's party and the Commons moved quickly — in removing the Tory whip and imposing a 10-day suspension from the Commons respectively — it took a Freedom of Information Act (FOIA) request from the *Daily Mirror* and a further 3-month delay to identify just what financial penalty had been imposed on the errant MP. On 28 July the paper reported that Conway was being asked to repay just £13,160 of the £45,163 said to have been given in salary to his youngest son — and that he would be allowed to return even this small proportion in 12 monthly instalments.

The case for the defence

In an interview with the *Mail on Sunday*, Mr Conway said: 'I still believe I have done nothing wrong.' He said that his son [Freddie] travelled down from Newcastle to help him with his MP's work.

He told the paper: 'I know many MPs with family members who have different names registered, so that they are not so obviously spotted. Some spouses work under maiden names.'

Mr Conway insisted that both Freddie, 22, and elder son Henry, 25, whom he employed earlier, did the work they were paid for. 'A lot of students do part-time work. He was working for his father rather than working in McDonald's,' he said. 'He used to come home frequently. There are MPs who commute greater distances than Freddie on a weekly basis. I don't think that it was unusual.'

Source: '"I'm no crook," says suspended MP', www.bbc.co.uk, 3 February 2008.

What is the additional costs allowance and why has it proven so controversial?

MPs' expenses averaged £136,000 per head (£88 million in total) for the tax year 2006/07 — a figure double that paid out in basic salaries. The basic salary for 2007/08, along with the upper limits for the various allowances payable, is shown in Table 7.2.

Salary	£61,820
Staffing allowance	£100,205
Incidental expenses provision (IEP)	£22,193
IT equipment (centrally provided)	£3,000
London supplement	£2,916
Additional costs allowance	£24,005
Communications allowance	£10,400
Total	**£224,539**

Source: House of Commons Research Paper 08/31.

Table 7.2 MPs' salaries and allowances at April 2008

The 'John Lewis' list

The alleged misuse of the additional costs allowance (ACA) — the sum provided for serving MPs to maintain a second home away from their constituency — received considerable media coverage in 2008. Particular attention was paid to the so-called 'John Lewis list' (see Table 7.3). This list, previously unknown even to most MPs, was essentially an administrative tool designed to help civil servants determine whether those expenses claimed by MPs were to be considered reasonable and, therefore, allowable. In essence, it consisted of a list of items that an MP might choose to claim for under the

ACA, along with a maximum allowable price drawn from the John Lewis stock list; hence the 'John Lewis list'. The media coverage of the list was, as former Conservative minister Anne Widdicombe noted, somewhat mischievous, as it gave the impression that MPs were going shopping with a view to spending up to the stated limit on anything from a new kitchen to an electric lamp. In reality, of course, members would probably only have been aware of the upper limit on each item if they had exceeded it. Indeed, some of the headline figures quoted were in themselves misleading. For example, the oft-quoted £10,000 allowance for a new kitchen would only have been payable in full if the whole kitchen was being replaced out of necessity, rather than for aesthetic reasons. Where the MP's motivation was deemed a combination of 'need' and 'taste', the allowable amount was to be reduced accordingly.

Kitchen fitting	£10,000
Bathroom fitting	£6,335
Suite of furniture	£2,000
Television	£750
Stereo system	£750
Rugs	£300
Food processor	£200
Electric lamp	£200
Coffee machine	£100
Fitted carpet with underlay	£48 per square metre

Source: 'Never knowingly undersold: the MP's guide to setting up home on expenses', *Guardian*, 14 March 2008.

Table 7.3 The John Lewis list (some highlights)

The Freedom of Information Act bites

In February, the Information Tribunal ruled against the efforts of Jack Straw and the Commons speaker Michael Martin to keep the details of MPs' expenses secret, concluding that:

> The laxity of and lack of clarity in the rules for ACA [additional costs allowance] is redolent of a culture very different from that which exists in the commercial sphere or in most other public sector organisations today. In our judgement these features, coupled with the very limited nature of the checks, constitute a recipe for confusion, inconsistency and the risk of misuse.

The details, which had originally been requested in a Freedom of Information Act (FOIA) request submitted by the Press Association, were eventually released at 4.30 p.m. on the afternoon of Thursday, 13 March 2008, although the deadline set had in fact been Monday, 10 March — a delay that brought widespread criticism (see Box 7.2).

In May, further requests under the FOIA (2000) resulted in the release of a further 450 documents relating to the ways in which 14 named MPs and a number of high-spending former MPs had used their additional costs allowance in recent years. As the *Guardian* reported on 24 May, the list of items claimed by the 14 was, to say the least, rather eclectic:

- John Prescott, it was revealed, had claimed £6,707.06 for external repairs to his Hull constituency home, including fixing mock-Tudor boards to the front gable. He had also claimed a further £2,880 on food to cover an 8-month period.
- Margaret Beckett had been granted £1,320 to cover the cost of constructing a pergola in the garden of her constituency home in Derby, although her claim for £600 worth of plants had been refused.
- David Cameron had claimed between £637.67 and £1,743.83 each month towards the mortgage for his London home.
- Gordon Brown had claimed £4,569.70 on refurbishing his property, £100 on a Sky subscription and £32 on lightbulbs — at a time when his salary as chancellor totalled £136,000 per annum.

The reaction to such revelations was widespread incredulity. Although some of the larger claims in respect of London accommodation were understandable, many failed to see why taxpayers' money should be used to make improvements to MPs' constituency homes or to cover minor items of everyday spending: the Liberal Democrat MP Mark Oaten, for example, had even claimed £5 for a pair of oven gloves. Matthew Elliott of the Taxpayers' Alliance appeared to catch the public mood when he said that 'taxpayers should not be made to pay for Gordon Brown's Sky TV subscription or Tony Blair's £10,000 kitchen'.

The obvious media appeal of the John Lewis list and the revelations regarding some of the smaller items claimed under the ACA served to relegate coverage of more serious abuses of allowances to the inside pages. This was particularly true in the case of those claiming some or all of the monthly mortgage costs payable in respect of their second homes. Even so, the behaviour of Sir

Nicholas Winterton and his wife Ann did hit the headlines. The Wintertons, it was reported, had put their £700,000 Belgravia flat (a property that they had owned outright since 2002) into trust, charged themselves £21,600 a year in rent and claimed this sum back from the taxpayer until they were prevented from doing so in 2008.

The coverage of such behaviour did little to enhance the reputation either of MPs themselves or of the Commons at a time when Westminster was still struggling to recover from the earlier scandals over party funding. Most worrying, however, was the fact that — Conway aside — most of the behaviour that was considered so shocking had taken place within the existing regulatory framework. As Ed Balls pointed out in a statement issued on Wednesday, 25 June, he and his wife (Yvette Cooper) had followed the rules laid down by the fees office.

For many, therefore, the events of 2008 appeared to echo those of a decade before, when the alleged indiscretions of Neil Hamilton and others over the 'cash for questions' scandal and the spectre of sleaze had done so much to damage the reputation of the Conservative Party.

Why didn't the Commons move more quickly to diffuse the situation?

Although the allegations surrounding the alleged misuse of MPs' expenses clearly damaged the reputations of those individual MPs targeted, the failure of the Commons to act quickly and decisively in the wake of the revelations only served to deepen public disquiet. The fact that the speaker, Michael Martin, the man who led the commission investigating possible impropriety, found himself and his wife caught up in allegations regarding the false claiming of expenses, did little to inspire confidence in his ability to look at the issue with an independent eye. It was no surprise, therefore, that the speaker's efforts to block the publication of MPs' expenses by resorting to High Court action was seen as part of a Commons cover-up. This was a great pity, as MPs did in fact have a number of genuine concerns regarding full disclosure:

- Many MPs regard their allowances as reasonable in light of the fact that their basic salary is lower than many members could earn in comparable posts outside of Parliament.
- There is a general sense that MPs should be able to claim some form of allowance when forced to live away from their primary residences for such lengthy periods.
- The most obvious solution, to sweep away the various allowances and pay MPs a far higher basic salary, would ignore the fact that different MPs have different levels of need. It is likely, for example, that the MP for Ross, Skye and Lochaber, Charles Kennedy, would have higher travel expenses and a greater need for a London home than one who lives in and represents a constituency within easy travelling distance of the capital.

- Many of those MPs who opposed the release of individual expenses had concerns regarding the way in which the release of information (in particular, their home addresses) might compromise their safety or subject them to unfair media scrutiny. In the case of the latter, many feared that the papers would focus on the headline expenses total for each MP, rather than look at whether such claims were warranted. As Birmingham Hodge Hill MP Liam Byrne had put it when challenged over his £28,170 postage claim, 'When I was elected I promised to stay in touch with my constituents and I intend to honour that pledge' (*Independent*, 26 October 2007).

Conclusions: what can be done to restore confidence in the integrity of our MPs?

There remains a fundamental conflict of interest at the heart of the issue of MPs' pay and allowances: namely, that it is the MPs themselves who ultimately determine the scope and scale of such payments, as well as the regulations that govern the way in which they are applied.

Box 7.3 **From 'John Lewis list' to 'IKEA list'**

MPs yesterday imposed an annual cap of £2,400 on household goods they can claim for their second homes. The Tories, who previously had called for an end to any furniture claims by MPs under the additional costs allowance (ACA), accused the government of treating voters like fools by replacing 'the John Lewis list with the IKEA list'.

Harriet Harman, the leader of the Commons, defended the decision to maintain the household goods allowance by taking a swipe at the Tories. 'I believe in equality. We believe that to be MPs we should not have to depend on private wealth to do our job.'

Source: *Guardian*, 17 July 2008.

As we have already noted, the obvious response to the furore over expenses would be simply to remove the various allowances and instead raise the basic salary for MPs to a level where members can fully cover their living costs. Ironically, however, it was the sheer unpalatability of paying MPs a six-figure headline salary that led to the rise of these less visible allowances in the first place. In a sense, therefore, the problem facing those who seek to reform MPs' expenses is the same as that facing those attempting to tackle the thorny issue of party funding: that of public perception. In short, there is a clear need for a candid and very public debate about just what kind of legislature we want to have and how we want it to be funded.

In the absence of such a frank and open debate, it is inevitable, perhaps, that changes to MPs' pay and conditions will be piecemeal in nature (see Box 7.3). That said, such changes should at least bring a greater degree of clarity to the system and, as freedom of information campaigner Heather Brooke commented in the *Guardian* on 26 June, 'Transparency is, and always has been, the main issue in relation to MPs' expenses.'

Summary

- 2008 saw intense scrutiny regarding the way in which MPs had been exploiting their parliamentary allowances.
- The Conway scandal focused attention on a system that had become increasingly out of touch with practice elsewhere in the public and private sectors.
- While most MPs were working well within the letter of the regulations, a significant number were exploiting their 'second home allowances' in a manner that was not entirely in keeping with the spirit of the law.
- The Commons made a number of minor changes to MPs' allowances in the autumn of 2008.
- More substantive progress is unlikely without a frank and open public debate over precisely what we want from our legislators and the manner in which they can be best rewarded for their services.

Chapter 8

Brown and constitutional reform: unfulfilled promise?

Context

In March 2008 the government published its draft Constitutional Renewal Bill (Cm 7342) — the legislation intended to carry into law many of the proposals outlined a year earlier in the *Governance of Britain* Green Paper (Cm 7170). Widely anticipated as Brown's blueprint for a new wave of constitutional reform, the original Green Paper had disappointed those expecting something more radical; the disparate and technical nature of the bill brought forward in 2008 meant that even many of those who had welcomed the Green Paper were left wondering whether or not there was any real point in proceeding.

This chapter examines the extent to which the Constitutional Renewal Bill represents a worthwhile use of what limited parliamentary time remains ahead of the next general election. In so doing it will consider issues such as:

- How well received was the draft Constitutional Renewal Bill?
- What kinds of change did the bill propose?
- Which areas of constitutional reform were omitted from the bill and why?

How well received was the draft Constitutional Renewal Bill?

Our 2008 survey delivered a fairly damning verdict on Brown's 2007 *Governance of Britain* Green Paper: 'Although the 63-page...Paper says a great deal', we concluded, 'few of its provisions are truly original, and those that are, are often of questionable merit.'

The initial reaction to the draft Constitutional Renewal Bill (Cm 7342), designed to bring the Green Paper's provisions into law, was no more encouraging. Lord Falconer delivered a withering attack on the proposals in May 2008 (see Box 8.1) and even the Constitution Unit — which had welcomed the thrust of the *Governance of Britain* proposals — had its reservations about how easy it would be to inspire much enthusiasm for the raft of proposals outlined in the draft bill. As the Constitution Unit concluded in the May 2008 issue of its *Monitor* newsletter, the very name of the bill was itself likely to mislead and disappoint; far better, they concluded, to have called it the 'Strengthening of Parliament Bill' or the 'Prerogative Powers and Miscellaneous Provisions Bill'.

> **Box 8.1** **Falconer on the warpath**
>
> Lord Falconer, the former Lord Chancellor, yesterday launched a scathing attack on Gordon Brown's plans to reform the constitution, describing his reform bill as 'trivial', 'containing nothing of significance' and 'sometimes designed to meet problems that do not exist'. He said that the legislation was pointless, adding 'it is better to describe it as the constitutional retreat bill than a constitutional renewal bill. I believe there is next to nothing of significance [in] this bill. It is like filling in time,' he said.
>
> Source: Patrick Wintour, 'Falconer savages Brown's trivial reform bill', *Guardian*, 22 May 2008.

The bill was published in three separate volumes totalling 266 pages: 70 pages outlining the scope of the bill (Cm 7342i); 98 being the White Paper itself (Cm 7342ii); and a further 98 offering an analysis of the consultation process that had been undertaken (Cm 7342iii). Although this was clearly a substantial body of work, it was hard to escape Falconer's conclusion that the bill was little more than a stalling exercise. The parliamentary joint committee that reported on the bill on 31 July certainly shared such concerns, struggling to find the bill's uniting theme, criticising its title and questioning the merit of many of the proposals contained therein — most notably, the changes to the roles of the Attorney General and the Lord Chancellor.

What kinds of change did the bill propose?

The original *Governance of Britain* Green Paper had four stated aims, as reiterated in the preamble to the bill brought forward in 2008:

- To invigorate our democracy;
- To clarify the role of Government, both central and local;
- To rebalance power between Parliament and the Government, and give Parliament more ability to hold the Government to account; and
- To work with the British people to achieve a stronger sense of what it means to be British.

After a consultation period that had seen the publication of five separate documents (see Box 8.2) and elicited 1,000 separate responses — both from members of the public and from other interested parties, ranging from the judiciary to charity groups — the bill brought forward proposals in six distinct areas:

- the legal status of protests in the vicinity of Parliament
- the role of the Attorney General
- the judicial appointments process
- the treaty power and the war power
- the core values of the civil service (which had been subject to consultation back in 2004)
- the flying of the Union flag

Protests in the vicinity of Parliament

The manner in which the 2005 Serious Organised Crime and Police Act (SOCPA) had been used to limit the right of citizens to assemble and protest peaceably in the vicinity of Parliament had made it the subject of widespread criticism. Indeed, even some of those who had supported attempts to use the Act as a means of removing the peace protester Brian Haw's peace camp on Parliament Square were shocked by its broader application — the criminalisation of virtually any protest, however small, which had not been formally approved by the police several weeks in advance. The Kafkaesque nature of SOCPA (2005) was, as we noted in the 2008 survey, parodied to great effect by comedian-come-activist Mark Thomas, who made his 'mass-lone protests' the subject of an hour-long stand-up routine, a Radio 4 documentary and — ultimately — a bestselling DVD, *Serious Organised Criminal*. Some even credited Thomas with the government's about-turn over SOCPA, first mooted in the *Governance of Britain* Green Paper and carried through into the 2008 bill (see Box 8.3).

> **Box 8.3** **Managing protest around Parliament**
>
> The Government proposes the repeal of sections 132–138 of the Serious Organised Crime and Police Act 2005. Repeal of these sections will remove the requirement to give notice of demonstrations in the designated area around Parliament. It will also remove the offence for such demonstrations to be held without the authorisation of the Metropolitan Police Commissioner.
>
> Source: *The Governance of Britain — Constitutional Renewal* (Cm 7342i)

The role of the Attorney General

As we saw in our 2008 survey, although the desire to reform the role of Attorney General arose from concerns over the impartiality of legal advice given regarding the legality of UK action in Iraq, the scope of the proposals was, in fact, far wider (see Box 8.4). Such changes were obviously also part of a broader move to bolster judicial independence in the face of perceived political interference.

Box 8.4 **The role of the Attorney General**

- The Government proposes to make it clear that the Attorney General may not give a direction to the prosecuting authorities in relation to an individual case.
- The requirement to obtain the consent of the Attorney General to a prosecution in certain cases will, in general, be transferred to prosecutors.
- The Attorney General's power to halt a trial prior to sentencing (*nolle prosequi*) will be abolished.
- The Attorney General will be required to report to Parliament on an annual basis on the exercise of the functions of the Attorney General.

Source: *The Governance of Britain — Constitutional Renewal* (Cm 7342i)

Judicial appointments

The 2008 bill suggests a number of minor technical changes to the composition of the Judicial Appointments Commission (JAC) and the way in which it operates. More significant, however, is the plan to reduce the role played by the Lord Chancellor and the prime minister in respect of judicial appointments (see Box 8.5).

Box 8.5 **Judicial appointments**

The Government proposes to reduce the role played by the Lord Chancellor in judicial appointments below the High Court and to remove the need for the Lord Chief Justice to consult or obtain the concurrence of the Lord Chancellor in exercising certain functions. The Government also proposes to remove the Prime Minister from the process for appointing Supreme Court judges.

Source: *The Governance of Britain — Constitutional Renewal* (Cm 7342i)

Under these proposals the Lord Chancellor will lose the right to reject or ask the JAC to reconsider its selections in the case of all vacancies below High Court level — other than on medical grounds. In a parallel move, the prime minister will be entirely removed from the judicial appointments process at all levels. Although the premier's role in judicial appointments had long been considered something of a formality, this was nonetheless a significant symbolic change.

The power to wage war and conclude treaties

One of the central themes of the *Governance of Britain* Green Paper had been the effort to check the prime minister's prerogative powers. In no area have such prerogative powers provoked more controversy in recent years than in the case of the power to conclude treaties and take the nation to war: the Constitutional Renewal Bill sought to address the former by establishing that a procedure under Parliament would be required to scrutinise treaties prior to their ratification (see Box 8.6); the latter was to be the subject of a House of Commons resolution, which would set out the steps that would have to be gone through before UK armed forces could be deployed in armed conflict.

Although these two proposals, even in tandem, clearly fell some way short of the kind of formal War Powers Act favoured by the Liberal Democrats and others, they were largely well received.

Box 8.6 Treaties and the war power

The Government proposes to formalise the procedure for Parliament to scrutinise treaties prior to ratification to ensure a treaty cannot be ratified unless a copy of it is laid before Parliament for a defined period of 21 sitting days.

On War Powers, the Government will propose a House of Commons resolution which sets out in detail the processes Parliament should follow in order to approve any commitment of Armed Forces into armed conflict. The resolution will define a clear role for Parliament in this most important of decisions, while ensuring our national security is not compromised.

Source: *The Governance of Britain — Constitutional Renewal* (Cm 7342i)

The core values of the civil service

The *Governance of Britain* Green Paper had suggested that the position of the civil service should be formalised, with its core values being enshrined in law and the civil service commissioners given a statutory footing. Such proposals, which built upon a government consultation paper of November 2004, were included in the 2008 bill. Crucially, the Civil Service Code (see Box 8.7) was, for the first time, to become part of the service's conditions of employment.

Box 8.7 The Civil Service Code

As a civil servant, you are appointed on merit on the basis of fair and open competition and are expected to carry out your role with dedication and a commitment to the Civil Service and its core values: integrity, honesty, objectivity and impartiality.

In this Code:

- 'integrity' is putting the obligations of public service above your own personal interests;

- 'honesty' is being truthful and open;
- 'objectivity' is basing your advice and decisions on rigorous analysis of the evidence; and
- 'impartiality' is acting solely according to the merits of the case and serving equally well Governments of different political persuasions.

Source: an extract from the Civil Service Code (2006).

Flying the flag

Given that so much of worth was left out of the bill, it was, perhaps, a little surprising that proposals to loosen the regulations governing when the Union flag could be flown on public buildings had made the final cut (see Box 8.8). More surprising still was the fact that this was the only significant measure to survive from section 4 of the *Governance of Britain* Green Paper, with more meaty proposals such as a British bill of rights having been left on the drawing board.

Box 8.8 | Flag days

On flying the Union Flag from public buildings the Government proposes to relax the restrictions that currently only allow the Flag to be flown on 18 designated days.

Source: *The Governance of Britain — Constitutional Renewal* (Cm 7342i)

Which areas of constitutional reform were omitted from the bill and why?

The *Governance of Britain* Green Paper had been divided into four broad sections:
1 Limiting the powers of the executive
2 Making the executive more accountable
3 Re-invigorating our democracy
4 Britain's future: the citizen and the state

However, the various consultation papers issued by the government in the wake of the Green Paper and the Constitutional Renewal Bill published in 2008 (see Box 8.2) focused almost entirely on measures outlined in the first two sections of the Green Paper.

In reality, the only significant change to survive from section 3 of the Green Paper was the plan to ease restrictions on protests in the vicinity of Parliament. Similarly, the only measure to survive from section 4 — as we have seen — was the decision to make it easier to fly the Union flag on public buildings. In essence, therefore, everything of substance that had appeared in the second half of the *Governance of Britain* Green Paper in 2007 was missing from the

Constitutional Renewal Bill published in March 2008. This included most of the things that one might expect to find in a bill worthy of such an auspicious title (see Box 8.9).

Box 8.9 What was missing?

- Lords reform
- Electoral reform
- All-women shortlists
- Weekend elections
- Petitions and e-democracy
- Bill of rights

Some of these areas were addressed by other means. Lords reform, for example, was the subject of a separate White Paper in July 2008. There was an obvious logic to adopting such a twin-track approach to constitutional reform. After all, there was clearly no advantage in delaying the proposals in the Constitutional Renewal Bill further by tying them to a programme of Lords reform that had already been put on ice until after the next general election. That notwithstanding, it was hard to escape the conclusion that the removal of Lords reform and the other more contentious proposals from the 2008 bill had ripped the heart out of what had in itself been a fairly modest Green Paper.

Conclusions

The original *Governance of Britain* Green Paper was a disparate mish-mash of initiatives; a crushing disappointment to those who had expected Brown to launch his premiership with an agenda that was truly groundbreaking. Despite its auspicious title, the Constitutional Renewal Bill was in many respects an even greater disappointment, because it focused almost entirely on taking forward the more marginal and technical changes outlined in the Green Paper, while leaving many of the proposals that might have truly captured the public imagination on the back-burner.

While it is perhaps inevitable that more intractable problems such as Lords reform and electoral reform will be the subject of separate legislation, the reality is that it is now nearly 12 years since New Labour drafted the manifesto that committed the party to a course of major constitutional reform. The party has now held power for more than a decade, its longest continuous period in office and a period in which Labour has enjoyed Commons majorities ranging from the serviceable (post-2005) to the overwhelming (1997–2005). With this state of affairs unlikely to continue after the next general election, time would appear to be running out for Labour's constitutional agenda; put simply, if not now, when?

Summary

- The original *Governance of Britain* Green Paper (2007) had been something of a disappointment to those who had expected Gordon Brown to mark the beginning of his premiership with something truly ground-breaking.

- The Constitutional Renewal Bill (2008) appeared purpose-built to disappoint even those who had come to accept the limited scope of the earlier Green Paper.

- Placing aside all talk of a 'British bill of rights' along with most of the other major proposals contained in the original Green Paper, the 2008 bill (Cm 7342) focused instead on a number of quite technical changes.

- Although such a 'tidying-up exercise' would have been widely welcomed, had it come in the wake of more substantive changes, critics questioned the intrinsic worth of the bill as published.

- Ironically, the bill's auspicious title only served to draw attention to all that it was not.

- Defeat for Labour at the next general election could leave its constitutional reform agenda high and dry.

Chapter 9

Multi-level governance in the UK: a road to nowhere?

Context

A generation ago, few would have argued that the UK was anything other than a unitary state. However, things have clearly changed in recent years. The widening and deepening of the European Union, the impact of New Labour's devolution programme and the proliferation of both elected and unelected regional bodies have all served to support the view that the UK is moving towards true multi-level governance.

This chapter considers some recent developments in the field of multi-level governance and identifies some of the challenges that lie ahead. In so doing it will consider issues such as:

- Lisbon and beyond — what next for the EU?
- Will devolution in Scotland inevitably end in the break-up of the Union?
- Whatever happened to the idea of regional government in England?

Lisbon and beyond — what next for the EU?

In our 2008 survey, we examined the similarities between the 2004 draft EU constitution and the 2007 EU Reform Treaty (now commonly referred to as the Lisbon Treaty), questioning whether or not UK citizens should have been offered the same referendum in respect of the latter that they had been promised in the case of the former.

By the start of 2008 that debate was effectively over, with the government having concluded that no referendum was necessary. Despite a sizeable Labour backbench rebellion, the Commons gave the treaty its approval on 5 March, by 311 votes to 248. The UK ultimately became the nineteenth EU member state to ratify the Lisbon Treaty, in spite of a last-ditch effort by millionaire Tory donor Stuart Wheeler to delay formal ratification of the treaty by forcing a judicial review.

Dealing with rejection

Although the UK's ratification of the Lisbon Treaty was a significant domestic event, there had been an important shift in the European political landscape even before the bill had received its royal assent on 20 June: the 'no' vote delivered by Irish voters in the referendum held on 12 June. Ireland was the only one of the 27 EU member states to offer its citizens an opportunity to vote on the treaty, and the post-mortem following the poll therefore provoked

heated debate across the continent. The Liberal Democrat MEP Andrew Duff was not alone in placing the blame for the setback at the door of the Irish government in Dublin, whose lacklustre campaign had made little headway in the face of a 'no' lobby comprising, as he put it, 'a toxic cocktail of anti-globalisers, neo-cons, the clergy and Trotskyists'. Although his remarks were not entirely wide of the mark, they quickly became irrelevant as the debate moved away from the question of *why* the Irish had rejected the Lisbon Treaty, towards a consideration of precisely *what* could be done to break the stalemate.

The pause for reflection that had followed the rejection of the draft EU constitution by voters in France and the Netherlands in 2005 had been criticised as all 'pause' and no 'reflection'. In effect, it took 2 years to find a way forward, with the EU Reform Treaty (the Lisbon Treaty) only being signed in December 2007. With all bar the Irish dismissing the call for a referendum on the ground that the new treaty was, in effect, only a tidying-up exercise, as opposed to a major constitutional proposal, success appeared guaranteed in 2008. The Irish setback was therefore all the more devastating for Europe's leaders. Some, including the German chancellor Angela Merkel, argued that there simply was not time for another 'pause for reflection'; others felt that such a pause was the only practicable response (see Box 9.1).

Box 9.1 The Irish referendum

The Irish government came under mounting pressure last night to stage a second referendum on the Lisbon Treaty. European leaders appeared divided over exactly how to proceed when they met in Brussels to respond to the defeat inflicted on their project last week by Irish voters.

The German chancellor Angela Merkel called for a quick response. 'We need the Lisbon Treaty', she said. 'Europe can't afford to have another phase of reflection.' One British official publicly disagreed, stating, 'We do need a period of reflection.'

Source: 'Ireland under pressure to vote again on treaty', *Guardian*, 20 June 2008.

Just how much trouble the treaty was in only became apparent when the French president, Nicolas Sarkozy, was heard praising the UK prime minister, Gordon Brown, for his courage in facing down opposition on the Labour back benches and completing UK ratification of the treaty. For the UK — so often characterised as Europe's 'awkward partner' — to be leading the charge must surely have only served to heighten the fears of those committed to the project from the outset. Such fears were realised when the 2-day summit of EU leaders in Brussels in June 2008 failed even to approve a formal statement committing all states bar Ireland to continue with their ratification of the treaty. The meeting ended with the prospect of the impasse not even being resolved ahead of the European Parliament election in June 2009.

Although the fate of the Lisbon Treaty is interesting in itself, it raises a far more important question: that of where precisely the EU is headed. The Union enlarged from 15 to 27 member states between 2004 and January 2007. Yet whenever referendums have afforded the general public the opportunity to offer a verdict on their leaders' vision for the future of the Union, the results have been at best inconclusive.

In the face of such rejection, Europe's political classes have, at times, appeared strangely out of step with the prevailing Zeitgeist, preferring to focus on how the masses might be persuaded of the merits of such schemes in a second referendum, or how the EU might instead implement as many of the changes as are practicable without the need for popular approval. While vision is a key characteristic of good government — leaders should, after all, lead — there was a growing sense in 2008 that it might finally be time to stop and listen. Although structural changes to the major EU institutions and processes are desperately needed in the wake of the unprecedented changes in the scope and size of the European Union, it might also be time to pause and take stock, with a view to developing and articulating a clearer sense of where the EU is ultimately headed: a union of sovereign member states or a United States of Europe.

Will devolution in Scotland inevitably end in the break-up of the Union?

6 May 2009 marks the tenth anniversary of the first elections to the Scottish Parliament. During their first decade in operation, the devolved institutions north of the border have generally been seen as one of the few success stories to emerge from the raft of constitutional reforms proposed in Labour's 1997 general election manifesto.

While some feared that devolution might merely serve to fuel demands for full independence, the reverse has in fact been the case. In reality, the halfway house of devolution appears to have satisfied the needs of most of those who yearned for greater autonomy, while at the same time offering the security of being part of a larger economic unit and a bigger player on the world stage. In spite of the fact that the SNP administration's approval rating hit 60% at the start of 2008, therefore, the proportion of Scots calling for full independence has fallen to only one in four. Indeed, those who do still hope for full independence are often seen as faintly anachronistic. As Channel 4's Stuart Cosgrove put it late in 2007, 'a lot of [the debate over independence] feels so arcane...The truth of the matter is, apart from some key institutions maybe it's already happened. That's the thing: Scotland already is independent, isn't it?'

While there would appear to be broad public approval for the way in which devolution has been implemented in Scotland, however, two crucial questions have yet to be satisfactorily addressed.

First, there is the question of representation — so famously framed in the West Lothian question (see Box 9.2). The reduction in the number of Scottish constituencies from 72 to 59 ahead of the 2005 general election went some way towards recognising the fact that most of the decisions that affect the everyday lives of Scots are now taken not at Westminster, but at Holyrood. However, such a mathematical adjustment does little to address the basic principle at the heart of the question.

Box 9.2 The West Lothian question

The phrase, 'the West Lothian question' was coined by Enoch Powell in the 1970s as a way of summing up the concerns of the then MP for the Scottish constituency of West Lothian, Tam Dalyell.

'For how long', Dalyell had asked in a Commons debate in 1977, 'will English constituencies and English Honourable Members tolerate...at least 119 Honourable Members from Scotland, Wales and Northern Ireland exercising an important, and probably often decisive, effect on British politics while they themselves have no say in the same matters in Scotland, Wales and Northern Ireland?'

Source: Oonagh Gay (2006) *The West Lothian Question*, Parliament and Constitution Centre.

Second, there are emergent differences in policy between different nations within the Union. While the decision not to press ahead with top-up fees and foundation hospitals north of the border caused a degree of consternation elsewhere in the UK — as had the Scots' provision of free nursing care for the elderly — such isolated policy differences have increasingly become the norm, rather than the exception, as the various devolved systems have diverged. In the case of National Health Service (NHS) provision, this has thrown up a number of realities which are, in the eyes of many onlookers, simply untenable: for example, the fact that by 2010 it is likely that all of the home nations bar England will offer free NHS prescriptions.

Such fundamentals are at the heart of many of the more petty stories garnering column inches in the press. The decision of the Westminster government to step in and bail out a number of failing banks — most notably the Royal Bank of Scotland and HBOS (Halifax Bank of Scotland) — is a case in point. Why, it was argued, should English taxpayers help to bail out Scottish banks? Although such arguments were easily rebutted — not least because both banks had a significant number of branches, employees and investors south of the border — there remains a popular perception of inequity in the post-devolution settlement between Scotland and England. Arguments (however well founded) about the scale and operation of the Barnett Formula (see Box 9.3) only serve to reinforce the view that those south of the border are being forced to subsidise a devolved Scottish administration that is providing better public services for its citizens. Such public unease may help to explain why the Conservatives and some others are so keen to address the funding issue and institute 'English votes for English laws' or some similar system at Westminster (see Box 9.4).

The Barnett Formula

Introduced in 1978 and named after the then Chief Secretary to the Treasury, Joel Barnett, the Barnett Formula is part of the mechanism under which government spending for Scotland, Wales and Northern Ireland is determined.

The Formula works on the basis that, as a default position, a change in public expenditure in one part of the UK will result in a similar change in other areas, in proportion to their population.

The Formula works only for changes in expenditure. It does not address expenditure as a whole or the relative needs of different areas.

The impact of the Formula is disputed. Although it should result in a gradual closing of the gap between per-capita expenditure in England and that in Scotland (the 'Barnett Squeeze'), the operation of the mechanism means that a declining Scottish population can cause the funding gap to widen.

Placing limits on Scottish MPs

A Conservative government would restrict the voting rights of Gordon Brown and other Scottish MPs at Westminster. Scottish MPs would be banned from taking part and voting in the line-by-line consideration of English parliamentary bills to end an anomaly which arose after the devolution of power to Edinburgh.

The proposals came from a report by the former Tory chancellor, Kenneth Clarke, who rejected the call from some in his party that Scottish MPs should be prevented from having any say at all over English bills. Instead, Scottish MPs would only be prevented from participating between the second and third reading of an English bill, i.e. during the committee and report stages.

Source: 'Conservatives plan to limit Scottish MPs' voting rights', *Guardian*, 2 July 2008.

As is the case in respect of the continuous widening and deepening of the EU, the main problem with Labour's devolution programme would appear to be that there is no pre-defined end-point — no clear goal. As Tam Dalyell predicted back in the 1970s, the internal flaws in the scheme were always likely to manifest themselves, irrespective of the initial public reaction to the changes made.

Whatever happened to the idea of regional government in England?

The decision of voters in the northeast to reject the chance to have their own regional assembly, in a referendum held in 2004, appeared to mark the death-knell for the notion of devolved government for the English regions.

In reality, however, regional government had already been established — albeit in a rather less conventional form. The Regional Development Agencies Act (1998) had already established nine English regional development agencies

(RDAs) alongside nine English regional assemblies (initially 'regional chambers'), which were designed to keep the more business-oriented RDAs abreast of public opinion. Of these regional assemblies, however, only the 25-member London Assembly is directly elected; the other eight consist of members appointed by elected local councils and regional stakeholders.

Critics argue that this lack of democratic accountability (see Box 9.5) is at the heart of what is wrong with the regional tier of government: that it is an unelected 'quangocracy', far removed from the kind of directly elected regional government offered by New Labour in their 2002 White Paper, *Your Region Your Choice*. Crucially, this original plan would have served not only to enhance local democracy, but also to address the concerns over representation arising from New Labour's devolution programme (i.e. the West Lothian question).

Box 9.5 Democratic deficit

It often falls to salaried officials to iron out difficulties between different levels of regional government, sometimes meeting in 'officers' groups' or 'executive groups' to decide the final balance of priorities.

The officials may themselves live outside the area involved and enjoy strong networks with their equivalents at 'higher' and 'lower' levels, sometimes through having worked previously in another authority.

It is worth emphasising that some of the key players, those within the regional bodies, may devote the whole of their time to these roles, compared with sub-regional staff for whom this is only part of their job. There is a tendency to lose democratic legitimacy to professionals.

Source: Alan Townsend (2005) *Multi-level Governance in England*, Durham University.

The future direction of government at this level is not entirely clear in the absence of such directly elected English regional assemblies. All that we do know is that the system is likely to become even less democratically accountable in the short term, with the government planning to abolish the eight English regional assemblies outside London in 2010 and to transfer most of their responsibilities to the RDAs themselves.

Conclusions

There remains a general consensus that the principle of *subsidiarity* should govern the operation of multi-level governance in the UK. The reality is, however, that while many of the individual changes introduced since 1997 have been broadly welcomed, there is no clear sense of precisely where it is all leading.

Key term
Subsidiarity: the principle that government should be administered at a level most appropriate to the task at hand.

The situation is further complicated both by the widening and deepening of the European project and by the fact that different parts of the UK are now operating under wildly different constitutional arrangements. While local government in the UK was never truly uniform, the creation of devolved bodies in Scotland, Wales, Northern Ireland and London has only served to confuse matters further. Although it is clear that the UK is moving away from a purely unitary model — in practice, if not in theory — it is not entirely clear what we are moving towards. In short, although some have clearly enjoyed the 'journey', the ultimate destination remains unknown.

Summary

- The Irish rejection of the Lisbon Treaty further delayed the implementation of changes designed to allow an enlarged EU to function efficiently.
- European leaders appeared uncertain as to how to proceed, with some wanting to forge ahead regardless, and others calling for a more meaningful 'pause for reflection' than that which had taken place in the wake of the rejection of the draft EU constitution in 2005.
- While devolution in Scotland has been widely judged a success, intrinsic problems remain: not least the West Lothian question and the public reaction to the differences in the provision of public services that have become apparent as the home nations have diverged.
- The quangocracy that has developed to fill the void left by the failure of plans to establish elected English regional assemblies does little to enhance local democracy or accountability.

Postscript

The extent of parliamentary privilege

The early weeks of December 2008 were dominated by the ongoing furore over the police investigation into alleged leaks by Home Office civil servant Christopher Galley to the Tory shadow immigration minister Damian Green. Mr Green, it emerged, had earlier been held by police for 9 hours: his Commons office and home had been searched; his computer and Blackberry mobile phone had been seized in evidence.

Media coverage of the raid initially focused on the conduct of the Commons Serjeant at Arms, Jill Pay, who had granted the police access to Mr Green's office, despite their not having a valid warrant. Thereafter, the spotlight quickly moved to Ms Pay's 'line manager' — the Commons speaker Michael Martin. Initially, Mr Martin had implied that the decision had been Ms Pay's alone, even going so far as to criticise the police for failing in their duty to inform Ms Pay that they required a warrant. Subsequently, it emerged that Mr Martin may, in fact, have known rather more about the raid than he had first been prepared to admit publicly.

Although experts on the UK constitution, such as Oxford University's Vernon Bogdanor, were quick to point out that the decision to search Mr Green's parliamentary office was neither an infringement of parliamentary privilege, nor evidence of an emergent police state, the broadsheets nonetheless devoted acres of newsprint to the story. MPs were similarly enthralled by the affair, with a number of members mischievously drawing parallels between the searching of Mr Green's office and the efforts of Charles I to personally arrest the five MPs who had opposed him in 1642: by implication, inviting comparisons between the courage of the then speaker, William Lenthall, who had refused to advise the king of the MPs whereabouts, and Mr Martin's apparent complicity in the Damian Green affair.

The events of November were certainly newsworthy, but the scale of media interest in the affair can, in part, be attributed to the continuing controversy surrounding the performance of the speaker. Mr Martin has long been the subject of coded criticism from the Conservative benches; the suggestion being that the one-time Labour member for Glasgow North East is not sufficiently impartial when discharging his duties from the speaker's chair. Mr Martin's questionable handling of the investigation into alleged abuses of MPs' expenses (see Chapter 7) had further damaged his standing in the eyes of many observers.

With Christopher Galley bailed to appear at a police station in January 2009 and Damian Green facing the prospect of further questioning a month later, the whole affair looked unlikely to simply fade away as 2008 drew to a close. Although calls for Mr Martin's resignation or even his impeachment had abated by the end of the year, the speaker's decision to hand-pick those charged with the task of investigating his involvement in the affair again raised questions over his judgement.

The Lisbon Treaty: does 'no' always mean 'no'?

In Chapter 9 we reported on the fallout that ensued from the Irish rejection of the Lisbon Treaty in a referendum held on 12 June 2008; noting that EU leaders were hoping that some solution might be found ahead of elections to the European Parliament in June 2009. By the middle of December, the path ahead had become somewhat clearer. On 5 December, the *Financial Times* reported that Ireland had set out its conditions for ratifying the treaty, whether through a second referendum or by some other means. These conditions included a guarantee of Ireland's right to nominate a EU commissioner, concessions on family law (specifically over abortion), control over their own tax rates and a guarantee of the nation's military neutrality. On 12 December 2008, it was announced that Ireland would indeed hold a second referendum in October 2009, after leaders attending a EU summit effectively agreed to Ireland's terms.

This is not the first time that the Irish people have been faced with a second referendum having failed to give the 'correct' response at the first time of asking. When the Irish rejected the Treaty of Nice in a referendum held on 7 June 2001, for example, the government brought forward a second referendum, campaigned more effectively, and secured a clear 'yes' vote on 19 October 2002. The case for a second referendum on the Lisbon Treaty was, if anything, even more compelling. After all, Ireland had been the only one of the 27 member states to consider it necessary to hold a referendum ahead of ratification. The Irish position was made weaker still by the fact that by 2009 they were likely to be the only member state not to have completed the ratification process. If the Irish had not agreed to a second referendum on Lisbon, therefore, they might have found themselves under pressure to hold a ballot on the question of whether they should even remain a full member of the Union.

Although the deepening economic crisis meant that Irish public opinion was already moving in the direction of a 'yes' vote by the close of 2008, the fact that citizens are being asked to 'think again' for a second time in under a decade does tend to undermine the value of such polls. After all, it is unthinkable that the Dublin government would have been calling for a second poll had they secured a 'yes' vote on 12 June.

The fallout from policing of the Climate Change Camp at Kingsnorth

Those protesting at Kingsnorth power station in August 2008 (see Chapter 6) had frequently complained about what they saw as heavy-handed policing. However, the government argued that the 70 injuries sustained by officers patrolling the Climate Change Camp were enough to justify both the police tactics and the £5.6 million cost of the security operation at the site.

On 15 December, however, the *Guardian* reported that this extensive police injury list was not entirely as it appeared. Evidence obtained by the Liberal Democrats under the Freedom of Information Act (2000) showed that there were in fact only 12 reportable injuries to officers during the protest, that only four of these incidents had involved direct contact with protesters, and that none of the four injuries was considered serious enough to warrant further action. According to the *Guardian*, the other reported injuries included: possible wasp stings; exhaustion caused by the sun and heat; cuts sustained while climbing fences or mending a car; and a back injury sustained when an officer used their leg to open a door. Other 'injuries' treated by the police 'tactical medicine unit', but not among the 12 reported cases, were said to include toothache, diarrhoea and bad headaches.

The relatively trivial nature of many of these injuries only served to focus attention back on the enormous cost of the policing operation. It also added credence to the protesters' claims that the authorities were trying to falsely brand them as 'dangerous' or 'violent' as a means of discrediting their campaign.

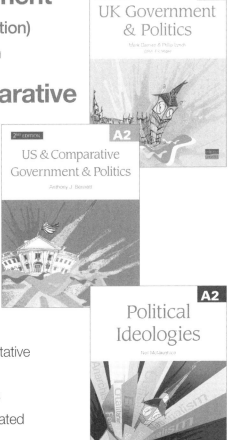